FUNDAMENTALS OF

CO-COUNSELING

MANUAL

(ELEMENTARY COUNSELORS MANUAL)

For

BEGINNING CLASSES IN

RE-EVALUATION COUNSELING

Rational Island Publishers
P.O. Box 2081, Main Office Station
Seattle, Washington 98111, USA

Manufactured in the United States of America

For information write to:

Rational Island Publishers
P.O. Box 2081, Main Office Station
Seattle, Washington 98111, U.S.A.

ISBN: 1-58429-073-0
$6.00

PREFACE to the Fourth Revised Edition

This is the Fourth Revised Edition of the English language version of the *Fundamentals of Co-Counseling Manual.* It contains significant additions to the theory of Re-evaluation Counseling, developed since the *Manual* was first written. A section was added in the Third Revised Edition in 1982. This section has been rewritten and additional theory has been included in it from Harvey Jackins' report to the 1981 World Conference. (The reports are printed in full in *The Reclaiming of Power.*) Harvey had planned on including this material.

A thorough re-writing of the *Fundamentals Manual* has been considered but is still being debated, so that decision must be delayed for at least another year.

The *Manual* is now also available in Arabic, Chinese, Croatian, Danish, Dutch, Farsi, French, German, Greek, Hebrew, Hungarian, Finnish, Indonesian, Japanese, Kannada, Kiswahili, Lithuanian, Russian, Shona, Spanish, Swedish, Tamil, and Telugu.

— Tim Jackins
February 2001

PREFACE to the Third Revised Edition

On this occasion of the umpteenth printing of the English language version of the *Fundamentals Manual* the question arises of whether to do a thorough revision of the text in the light of our growing knowledge, wider perspectives, and vastly expanded experiences of Re-evaluation Counseling in many cultures. Certainly each Fundamentals student deserves, for example, to be told (as we could say clearly earlier) that his or her skill as a counselor is a function not only of his or her progress as a client, and integration of the theory into life, but also of a *decision* and commitment to achieve the client's re-emergence.

The decision is not to drastically revise, however, at least not at this time. The material in the *Manual* is so trim and *workable* that every beginning Co-Counselor should be exposed to it. What I have done, instead, in order to give new Co-Counselors early exposure to some of the current viewpoints of basic theory is to *add*, on pages 43-54, the portions of the main report to the 1981 World Conference dealing with fundamental theory and a "fresh look" summary presented to a "new audience" in November of 1981.

The *Manual* is now available also in Chinese, Danish, Dutch, French, German, Greek, Hebrew, Kannada, Swedish, and Telegu translations.

— Harvey Jackins
April 1982

PREFACE to the Second Revised Edition

This edition has been revised to eliminate the use of the masculine gender pronouns as if they were the common gender, a usage that has, in the last few years, come to be understood as sexist and discriminatory.

— Harvey Jackins
September 1975

PREFACE to the Revised Edition

This *Manual* is the "workhorse" of Re-evaluation Counseling literature. Many thousands of today's Co-Counselors began their Co-Counseling in elementary classes with this *Manual* as their textbook. It is still without peer as an explicit guide to the basic business of making counseling work.

This revised edition includes a number of refinements in language and some small additions. The sturdier binding will be welcomed by those Co-Counselors who have "worn out" their copies of the original edition.

— Harvey Jackins
December 1970

BECOMING A COUNSELOR

It's not difficult to be a Re-evaluation Counselor, and yet in a way it's very difficult.

What you'll have to do will be a fairly simple matter, once the theory and practice is understood, and yet doing it will often be complicated.

What It Consists Of

What you will be doing is assisting another person to become free of rigid patterns of behaving and feeling which have been left upon him or her by experiences of being hurt in the past. The only serious and persistent difficulties in your way will be the rigid patterns which have been left upon *you.*

Teamwork

You and the client whom you are going to help will team up together. The client will use his or her flexible, non-rigid thinking.

With some very precise assistance from you, your client will become able to discharge, release and be freed of stored up tensions which have held his or her patterns of hurt in place and then think through the experiences of hurt until she makes complete sense of them. Then the experience will no longer affect her in rigid or compelling ways, but only as if they were ordinary memories of ordinary living.

THE ORIGIN OF TROUBLES

Each time your client was hurt, he lived through the experience and stored up in some way everything that went on during that experience of being hurt. He stored all the sights and sounds and smells and characters and conversations; the grief or anxiety or anger or pain, and, recorded right in with the rest, a shutdown of his ability to think, since human beings do not think in a sensible, rational way while they are being hurt.

Your client has tried to think through the stored up experience by himself repeatedly, has tried to make sense of it, but has always been balked in getting more than the edges of the experience because to think about it is to experience the inability to think which came with the original pain or painful emotion.

INHERENT HEALING PROCESSES

After being hurt, an infant will cry loudly and continuously and, if permitted to do so, will seem to recover from the hurt very quickly. After being frightened badly, an infant will scream and shake and perspire. After being angered, a yelling, vigorous tantrum will result, unless interfered with by others in the vicinity. A child, given friendly attention after an embarrassing situation, will talk and laugh about the experience spontaneously until the embarrassment is dissipated. These discharges — the crying, the trembling, the angry shouting, the laughter — are the ways in which human beings release the tensions which the experiences of hurt place upon them.

Apparently babies — given a chance — would keep themselves free from hurts simply by their natural discharge of painful emotion. In our culture, no baby gets very much of a chance because, with sympathy or with harshness, the discharge of her painful emotion is interfered with and shut off so repeatedly that to shut it off becomes an automatic pattern accompanying the hurt.

Discharges Are Not Hurts

There is a fundamental mistake in the ordinary thinking about these discharges. In our culture, tears are usually taken to mean grief. Trembling is taken to mean terror. Angry shouting is taken to mean anger. Therefore, it is thought that to shut off these discharges is to free a person from the emotion. "If you can stop them from crying, they won't feel bad. . . ." This is fundamentally backward.

The profound process of discharge of which tears are the outward indication is the getting over of grief. Tears indicate freeing one's self from grief. Crying never occurs unless a person needs to do it. In the same way, trembling and cold perspiration indicate the *release* of terror. Laughter accompanies becoming unafraid or un-irritated. Shouting and violent movement accompany becoming un-furious.

Grief

These means of release of tension occur in a certain order with human beings. What seems to be the heaviest and most profound of the emotional hurts which we experience, we usually call grief. It discharges with tears and sobbing. If a person cries reviewing a very severe incident of hurt, she will cry again on repeated reviewing of the experience, but a point eventually will be reached where there are no more tears.

Fears

Repeated recounting will then lead typically to trembling, teeth chattering, shivering, and cold perspiration.

On exhaustion of all the trembling by repeated recountings of the experience, it will be succeeded by intense laughter as the lighter variety of fears release.

Angers

When this is over, repeating the story will bring a kind of discharge involving loud words or sounds, physical movement and warm perspiration. We are familiar with this as a "tantrum" or "blowing one's top."

This will pass and the lighter side of anger and irritation will discharge with laughter.

Boredoms

When this is through, certain phenomena seem to take place to release what we might call the painful emotion of boredom, with interested talking the outstanding manifestation.

First, there is a reluctance to recount the experience, then a springing forth of a wealth of detail newly remembered, and finally, laughter again as the experience becomes vague and "unimportant."

The person passes into a tone of zest, or freedom from painful emotion.

Basic Order

This series of means of discharge are very precise and seem to be common to all human beings, even though some may be shut off by the pattern of hurt experiences and their order may be obscured. They have been observed occurring (see page 9) in several thousand human beings to date.

We might note that each of these discharges of painful emotion involves a physical process.

Physical Hurts

There is another kind of stored-up tension which discharges too, but in a somewhat different manner. The tensions of physical discomfort, i.e., ill health, pain, muscle strain, hormone imbalance, anaesthesia, unconsciousness, etc., are usually found surrounded by painful emotion and act as a kind of core or foundation for the emotional distresses.

When the painful emotion discharges which we have described above have been completed, then these root tensions of the physical discomfort kind will be available to discharge. This discharge is indicated by yawning and sometimes by stretching and scratching. This level of discharge is no less important than the discharge of painful emotion, but it does not occur well until all or nearly all of the painful emotion has been discharged from a particular series of experiences.

Neither client nor counselor should seek to *direct* attention to these *physical* distresses. They can be restimulated in this way and cause the client prolonged discomfort, but they will not, in general, discharge under such conditions. (The only apparent exception to this, in the case of new physical hurts which just occurred, is discussed on pages 30, 31, and 32.)

Instead, counseling should be aimed at the discharge of the *emotional* distresses. When such discharge has proceeded far enough, yawns will spontaneously begin to interrupt the tears, tremblings, or other emotional discharge. The same phrase or direction which has been bringing tremblings, for example, will bring trembling followed by a yawn, and later, will bring one or more yawns every time its utterance is attempted.

Yawning (with or without stretching or scratching) can be as intense and prolonged a discharge as any emotional discharge. Huge, deep yawns may follow one another with great rapidity. The client can hardly close her mouth on one yawn before another is forcing its way out. Such a discharge will sometimes last for hours.

Because the "exciting" feelings of emotional discharge are absent or diminished during yawns, a client may feel during her first experience with this kind of discharge that she should go onto "something more important."

The counselor should reassure the client and persist with the yawns as long as possible. The most profound and permanent relaxation of old tensions and somatics and the deepest re-evaluation often follow these intense yawning sessions.

DISCHARGE INDICATIONS AND SEQUENCE CHART

"Kind" of Painful Emotion and Tension		Manifestation During Discharge
ZEST (absence of Painful Emotion)	⇧	Happy relaxation, turning of attention away from experience of hurt.
BOREDOM	⇧	Laughter Animated Talking Reluctant Talking
LIGHT ANGERS	⇧	Laughter, warm perspiration
HEAVY ANGERS	⇧	Angry noises, violent movements, warm perspiration
LIGHT FEARS (Embarrassments)		Laughter, cold perspiration
HEAVY FEARS	⇧	Trembling, shivering, cold perspiration, active kidneys
GRIEFS	⇧	Tears, sobbing
PHYSICAL PAINS AND TENSIONS		Yawns, stretching, scratching

The client will begin substantial discharge as close to the bottom of the painful emotion part of this chart as the tensions exist in that particular pattern and/or as he is able to discharge and will then tend to move upward on the chart as regularly as his particular discharge-inhibiting patterns permit.

HOW TO BEGIN

What can you do to help your client become free of rigid patterns of tension, patterns of behavior which cause trouble and prevent success?

Listening

The first thing you must do and do very well is to listen . . . listen with interest, with full attention.

If you will listen in this manner, your client will be encouraged and enabled to talk about himself, about his patterns of distress. He may relate them to you in terms of difficulties or he may relate them as experiences that occurred.

Many light tensions seem able to be unraveled because your client is enabled to think about them much more thoroughly if he or she can talk about them to an interested listener.

Asking Questions

The second thing you can do to help your client is to ask questions.

These questions are not designed to obtain information for you as counselor, although the client may think that is the point. These questions are

First: To reassure the client of your interest;

Second: To steer and guide her attention.

Permit and Encourage Discharge

Much of the time with your client will be spent seeking an opportunity for her to discharge emotional or physical tension in one or more of the precise ways we've discussed above.

You will be directing your client's attention to where such discharge is likely to occur and will encourage the discharge if it begins to shows signs of being able to begin. When discharge slows or stops, you will persist time after time with directing the client's attention once more to the point where the discharge can continue.

THINGS NOT TO DO

Almost all of the things for you NOT to do as a counselor will come under the general heading of: DON'T let the Client's Troubles Bother You. This, of course, is much easier said than done. This is the problem which you will never completely solve but which will improve as you work at it through your own counseling.

However, some particular things can be watched for.

Don't be Suggestive

Refrain from telling your client what you think of his problem.

Don't tell her of similar problems you have or that you know of.

Don't interpret for your client.

Don't give him "good advice" or point out answers. Answers are no good to him unless *he has worked them out himself,* and yours will only constitute a barrier to working out his own.

Try to spend your time listening . . . NOT talking.

Don't React Emotionally

The only correct attitude toward your client's problem is one of interest and relaxed concern. Indifference on your part will make you quite ineffective, but so will hostility or any other kind of emotional upset.

Equally as true, any kind of sympathetic response from you will constitute an obstacle to a person's handling his own problem. If you "sympathize" with a client's problem, you will be reacting out of your own stored problems and the client will feel this and be inhibited by it.

Don't Interrupt Discharge

When a client is discharging, don't interfere. You will often feel moved to help him accelerate or deepen the discharge, and this is sometimes possible. Be very perceptive to the results of what you do, however, and if there is any slackening of discharge, stop what you *are* doing and return to what you *were* doing.

Be Courteous

Avoid any appearance of discourtesy in the keeping of appointments, in manners and attitudes, in tone of voice. A client — even an amateur client — is placing great trust and confidence in anyone he accepts as a counselor and is most sensitive to any kind of offense.

Who Decides What to Work On?

It will be unworkable for you to approach your client with any preconceived notion of what she should work on or what is available. Sometimes you will have a rough idea from preceding sessions, but even then your insight will be limited as to what is the actual availability and readiness of material for counseling.

A client can always in some way bring to light the thing that needs to be worked on. She may tell you directly, having thought about it ahead of time. She may seem to be at a loss, and yet, given an opportunity to talk under her own direction (tell the story of her life, or such), she will eventually bring up the topic which will show signs of agitation, indicating the need for emotional discharge.

Whose Job to Keep at It?

Once having found material available and ready to be worked on, however, a client cannot be expected to break through into discharge by himself nor to stay with the material for repeated recountings that will make sufficient discharge possible.

Here it becomes *your* responsibility as counselor to keep returning the attention of your client to the point of emotional discharge over and over until a thorough job can be accomplished. You will do this even when the client seems to be making great efforts to distract himself and you away from the material.

WHAT RE-EVALUATION CONSISTS OF

Re-evaluation of a person's rigid patterns of behavior seems to consist primarily of his exploring these patterns with part of his attention, while at the same time managing with part of his attention to stay outside the pattern and achieving some kind of objective look at them.

This division of attention, this *balancing* of *attention between* the *content* of the *reactive pattern* or the experience of *hurt* and the *real world of the present*, seems to be necessary at every level of this process. It is present in the discharge of deep grief, it is present at every level up through the "talking out" of boredom.

Spontaneous Process

Actually these processes of re-evaluation (including all levels of discharge) take place *spontaneously* whenever such a division of a person's attention is achieved. If a person is thinking about an old grief but at the same is partly aware of the present situation which does not contain loss but is secure and includes the presence of a strong, concerned person such as the counselor, then tears will begin to flow.

Achieve Balance

On latent material — that is, material that is not chronically in restimulation but shows only when specifically restimulated by an unusual set of circumstances in the environment — you as counselor will usually have the problem of directing part of your client's attention to this material, so that a balance can be achieved.

In dealing with chronically restimulated material, however, you, as the counselor, will have what seems to be the opposite problem — to draw enough attention of your client *away* from the material, so that he or she can feel secure enough for discharge to take place.

Acute Restimulation

When a person is "upset" more than ordinarily by a happening in the environment, you, as counselor, can usually turn her attention to you or any second person and have her talk about the upset. This will attract enough attention outside of her restimulation and gain enough feeling of security and objectivity for her discharge to begin immediately.

Thus, a person coming home from work in a turmoil can often be handled by some interested listening and questioning. A little discharge will be followed by a quick rise in tone, as the temporary involvement in the pattern of upset recedes and some of the restimulated charge runs off.

Chronic Restimulation

With the material which has become chronically restimulated in a client, however, it becomes a very difficult matter to draw any of the client's attention outside the pattern. This pattern has been lived with so long that it has become "adjusted to." What rational behavior goes on (and there is likely to be quite as much of it as with any other person) is nevertheless constrained and modified by the rigid framework of the patterns which are in chronic restimulation. (We may note these in other people and refer to them as "little idiosyncrasies.")

Often it will be hard to make a satisfactory attack on these chronic patterns until considerable work has been done on more readily available material which has not yet been so "adjusted to" or which is in restimulation only sporadically.

The Deeply Disturbed Person

With the deeply disturbed person, material has been restimulated so continually and so deeply that you are faced with a very real problem in securing any free attention outside the patterns of aberration at all.

If little or no free attention is available, then your first approach to helping such a person must necessarily involve attracting attention *away* from the rigid patterns, out to the present environment or to pleasant memories.

Since there are few easily observable or dependable signals as to how much free attention a person may have, either chronically or acutely, counseling can always, with profit, begin with these lightest of techniques.

Free Attention Versus Aberration Depth

Because any of the patterns of hurt which are stored up by a client will clutch on to and soak up amounts of free attention in proportion to the depth of the painful emotion contained within them, you will always seek to direct your client's attention toward such material as will not swamp it but rather can be handled by it.

SPECTRUM OF TECHNIQUES

If the ways of working on your client's problem are arranged in the order of increasing demand on his or her attention, you will have understandable framework on which to work.

The advantages of this procedure are many:

First, you can begin with any client at the lightest technique level, work effectively there, and progress to a heavier or more demanding technique in series only when each previous one has worked satisfactorily. You can then feel quite able to retreat to the preceding technique if any given level proves unworkable. In this manner, the risks of over-restimulation can be kept very low. Any over-investment of attention that occurs can be gotten away from quickly.

PRESENT TIME TECHNIQUES

1. *Attention to the Counselor*

Attracting attention to what is going on at the present moment is the lightest and easiest way to help a client. The first such direction of attention will be to you, the counselor. With a client not deeply involved, a simple greeting *which gains a response* will often suffice. You can see that this technique is workable and can be passed to try the next heavier one.

With a deeply disturbed person, however, this very step of gaining some attention to you and beginning communication may be a long arduous task and one taxing your ingenuity to accomplish.

2. *Calling Attention to the Environment*

Once in communication with you, additional attention of your client may be invited to the environment. This may be done by simple direction, by questions, by engaging the client in activity which demands his attention, by requesting his opinion or judgment about present factors, and in other ways.

Every bit of extroverted attention won in this way from the client's preoccupation with his tension patterns is a real gain in rationality, in well-being, and in ability to be counseled at a heavier level. Attention freed in this way is subject to becoming lost again through restimulation, of course, but while free it can be used to make permanent gains.

A variation here is the little "game" of having a client attempt to be aware of as many details of his environment at once as possible. Done well, this will often "de-stimulate" a headache tension pattern in a few minutes by calling attention away from it.

3. *Making the Environment Interesting*

The third approach you can use on a present time level is to change your client's environment so that is worth paying some attention to. Such changes not only will tend to drop restimulative factors out by the very fact of change, but will positively attract attention away from introversion or aberration. It is much easier to pay attention to a work therapy shop than to a padded cell. It is easier to extrovert to a symphony or a beautiful park than to the faded wallpaper of a dingy bedroom.

REMEMBERING TECHNIQUES

1. *Remembering Pleasant Things*

Remembering is the lightest use of free attention to the past. It should begin with light, easy memories.

For a client to remember a fact about the past (just any untense fact) is an achievement, however small, and will have some good effect. To remember successful or pleasant things will have more effect in pulling attention away from the tension patterns.

2. *Moving Quickly to Different Kinds of Memories*

When working on a remembering level, each question should be directed to a different kind of memory. The questions can be phrased in groups to ask for *ordinary* memories, memories of *rational activity*, memories of successes, or pleasant memories, roughly in that order as the client's ability to remember improves.

Unless the change of topic is followed, incidents remembered may turn out to be (or lead into) incidents of severe tension which are more than the client is able to evaluate at the time. In that case, the free attention will become bogged, requiring beginning over with the lighter techniques.

3. *Remembering Little Upsets*

This procedure of quick, random remembering will also work on small incidents of upset, i.e., little experiences which are upsetting primarily because they restimulate earlier tensions. If the client is asked questions about little upsets, moving from one type to another quickly and not dwelling long on each, considerable evaluation will take place. Short bursts of laughter will often occur and the release of tension and the re-evaluation of experiences will proceed in small increments.

You are now beginning to tackle the stored up tensions of the client but still on a light level, still moving swiftly from incident to incident lest any one of them be so heavy as to engulf and bog all the free attention of the client. Even with a client who is able to handle heavier techniques, you will usually start a session by asking, "What good happened to you last week?" and after he has narrated that, then, "Any upsets last week?" He will run over on memory level the little restimulations of the week and so clear his attention for working at the heavier techniques for which he is then prepared.

4. *From Random to Similar*

Remembering by the client does not demand a very large amount of free attention to be successful but in its lightest form will require a random kind of shift from one kind of memory to another, not allowing the client's attention to stay in one kind of incident or in one area very much. This will keep the attention from being over-engaged in too heavy material onto which you happen accidentally or which becomes restimulated.

It is possible to apply remembering to *similar* incidents. When this is done to a series of incidents, more attention is required on the part of the client for it to be successful.

5. *Rapid Review or Scanning*

With enough free attention available, it becomes possible to have the client do a kind of a rapid review through a series of similar experiences (what is often called "scanning"). Here the client is asked for the earliest available memory of a certain kind and then reviews later similar experiences in roughly chronological order all the way up to the present. Repeating, he begins once more at the earliest experience of this kind that is remembered and reviews the list again to the present. This will be done over many times.

The client can review such a chain of experiences mentally without talking about them, but the ability of the counselor to be aware enough of what is going on so as to be able to help and steer is limited by such a silent review. A combination of talking and silently reviewing material seems to work well and rapidly.

In this, the client recounts verbally all the experiences as he or she first remembers them, but on repetition of the series, reviews the ones that have already been mentioned silently and verbalizes only on the new incidents as they show up. In this way, a very large number of experiences of a certain type, most of which are restimulations of the same patterns, can be reviewed in a short period of time. Discharge may occur with the verbalization or even with the silent reviews, and the short bursts of laughter or angry exclamations will not interfere or slow down the reviewing process.

Also, the experiences which were first remembered will drop off the list on repeated viewings, i.e., they will seem to become forgotten or mislaid. The actual process apparently is that they become enough evaluated that the identification with that particular pattern is broken.

Finally the series of experiences will seem to have been reviewed to the point where it is difficult to remember them any more. Sometimes clients will say, "They have all faded." They will begin to talk about new experiences which are the reverse of the original category; i.e., someone who has been reviewing the times when "father was mean" will begin to talk about the times when "father was kind." Sometimes the client will persistently go to a new topic and begin reviewing experiences on that topic instead of being able to stay with the one you have been going over any longer. All these are indications that the series chain has been reviewed as far as it can be at this time, that you are through with this technique.

Some Will Not Fade

Some of the experiences in the series which you are reviewing are likely to be so full of tension that they will begin to loom larger and larger to the client as they are reviewed. Sometimes the client will say he is unable to think of anything else except this one experience. Sometimes she or he will be able at the counselor's request to "go around" that one and leave it off the list.

If the client is able to discharge emotion well and begins to discharge on one of these large experiences, then you may proceed in that direction, but you should realize that you are moving to a heavier technique away from the comparatively light reviewing.

Special Advantages

There are many special advantages to this technique because it allows the client's attention to travel without additional direction all the way from the earliest experience on the chain to present time. It permits certain of the client's mental abilities to operate freely and to sort out the list of significant experiences with great accuracy and precision. Thorough scanning out of a chain attached to the particular symptom or difficulty of a client will present the material that needs to be evaluated in order to relieve that symptom very, very accurately. Sometimes the difficulty can be keyed out in a most dramatic fashion simply by the scanning process itself. Where this is not sufficient, however, the remaining incidents are dug out and presented to view for evaluation with heavier techniques.

Regaining of Knowledge

Another unusual advantage of this is in the recovery of occluded or lost information. Educational courses, skills, languages, which were once usable by the client or which he/she studied can be brought to light and made once again usable by this repetitive review. Much of the information in school courses is often taken in by a student at the level of boredom and can be dusted off and actually come to be understood for the first time by this process.

To do this, simply begin at the beginning of the course; have the client relate every single thing he remembers, every detail, every scrap of information, every experience, every upset, that occurred in connection with this course from the beginning right up to present time and then on repetition have him review the things he's already mentioned silently, speaking only on the new material that comes to mind. Continue repetitively until the entire series is vague or until heavier techniques are indicated for the experiences which are left.

THOROUGH DISCHARGE TECHNIQUES

Sustained Discharge Counseling

Beyond reviewing lie the techniques of heavy discharge. Here the sustained physical discharge of painful emotion is sought and obtained and persisted with to the exhaustion of the tension stored in the experience. How demanding these techniques are upon the client's free attention is a variable thing — depending on the intensity and degree of hurt contained in the particular experience.

Discharge is Spontaneous

In the material which a client talks about, it will not always be obvious what level of discharge is necessary to relieve the tension spoken of. People have their own subjective names for their painful emotion and until the discharge begins, you as counselor will be uncertain of what it is going to be. Tension will show up as the attention of the client dwells on one of these experiences. A counselor's concern will be to secure its discharge, not to decide what level of discharge is needed.

Level of Discharge Not the Same as Importance

Because tears are the heaviest of painful emotion discharges, and because tears are not resorted to as commonly in our culture as laughter, for example, there is often a tendency for the beginning counselor to feel that only the discharge of grief is important; that if a client laughs or talks angrily, she is "avoiding" the "real" tensions which she has and which should be discharged in tears.

The discharge of grief is extremely important and it is proper for a counselor to seek ways to help the client unload the griefs she is carrying. That does not mean, however, it is to be sought at the expense of any of the other kinds of discharge. If your client is discharging in laughter, you can feel very relaxed and calm about what is going on because a good job is being done and the grief discharges will come in their turn.

Any kind of emotional discharge — whether it is interested, non-repetitive talking, angry talking, storming, laughter, trembling, or tears — should be persisted in by repeatedly redirecting the client's attention to the material which brings it.

When ready, the discharge itself will break over into another form. This will happen: a person who is laughing hard, if interfered with by a wrong attempt to get the "important tears," will not keep laughing well nor will he cry, but a person encouraged to continue with the laughter by the usual techniques will laugh harder and harder and then burst (possibly after a slight tense pause, possibly directly) into tears.

OVERCOMING PATTERNS WHICH INHIBIT DISCHARGE

The amount and resistance of the barriers to emotional discharge which any particular client has accumulated will vary greatly. One client will go into a full-scale discharge of tears, laughter, anger or heavy fear, in response to the initial question, "What's the problem?" Another may seem perfectly calm and controlled, and incapable of releasing any tension under the most favorable conditions. In the second case, of course, the person has been so thoroughly interfered with in tense situations in childhood as to have adopted as his own, compulsively, the holding in of his discharges under conditions of tension. He is in the position of a person rolled tightly in a ball of string. He can help the counselor get him out of the inhibition or controls only very little at first. He needs much skill, understanding, and patience, operating from the outside.

In all cases, however, the basic rule will apply: if the free attention of a person can be balanced between present-time, secure, unpainful reality AND the distressing experience pattern, then discharge will tend to occur spontaneously.

Outwitting the Control Pattern

Since the ways in which a person has come to hold in his painful emotion were ways that were developed during experiences of tension, then these "control patterns" are themselves necessarily rigid. For the spontaneous process of emotional discharge to be inhibited, these particular behaviors must be resorted to. When a client is in the position of having part of her attention in the tense material and part in the reassuring reality of present time, then *either emotion will spontaneously discharge or a control pattern must be in operation.* This control pattern will consist, in part, of the things that you observe the client doing at this time, and, since it is rigid, you can be of great help to your client by asking her to change what she is doing in some way so as to disturb or break up the rigidity of the way she is acting.

One client, for example, may talk with furious rapidity in such a situation. If you request and insist on slow repetition of one tense thought over and over, the fast-talking control pattern will be interrupted and discharge will probably occur.

Another client, caught in a control pattern of embarrassment, will hook her feet tightly together, grip the arm of the chair, hold her head back. If you ask such a person to uncross her feet, swing her arms in a relaxed manner, and put her chin on her chest as she talks about this tension, discharge is likely to begin as the rigid control pattern is interrupted.

Another client may be "composed," i.e., holding herself stiffly at attention in a facsimile of relaxation. The counselor may show such a person how to jitter visibly, pretend to chew at her fingertips, wiggle her feet, and do other nervous mannerisms which other people resort to. The thought of doing it will interrupt the rigid control pattern and discharge again is likely to occur spontaneously.

Validation

Because almost everyone has been hurt in situations where he has been ridiculed, belittled or downgraded, your client is nearly certain to have some kind of a chronic pattern of invalidating himself.

To contradict this pattern by encouraging your client to validate himself is an easy, safe way to begin effective counseling. Asking your client to praise himself will bring the "kickback" of the particular negative feelings of his pattern, and when these are *specifically* contradicted, discharge will occur freely.

For example, you may ask your man client to tell you in a sincere voice that he is the "handsomest, smartest and kindest hero in the world." If he tries, his invalidation pattern will compel him immediately afterwards to say that "he never figured he was very smart," for instance. At this point you know that you want him to concentrate on praising his intelligence for the largest amount of discharge.

A woman client who "wishes she were smart" should be put to work telling you in a happy voice that she is an "intelligent woman." (Her intelligence will begin to be more functional as soon as she begins to discharge.)

Emotional Discharge Undeliberate

Discharge can very seldom be a deliberate process. The client is directed to do something else — to tell the story of the emotional event, to repeat the poignant phrase, to answer the crucial question — and as he tries to do this, the discharge begins spontaneously.

Occasionally, the counselor will apparently direct the client to discharge emotion but it will be a pseudo-direction, intended to allow a spontaneous discharge of a different kind than that "asked" for.

Thus, the counselor might ask the client to use a sad face and a sad voice to describe an event, and long laughter discharge might ensue each time he attempts to do so. In so doing, your client avoids the control pattern for holding in the fear discharge (laughter) which is available.

Sometimes, too, discharge can be reached by having a client "go through the motions." Shaking a fist and shouting an angry phrase repeatedly is not of itself an anger discharge, but it is very likely to permit a real anger discharge to emerge if that level of anger is being suppressed. Similarly, to have the client deliberately and repeatedly shudder while talking about an incident of terror will not be a discharge itself, but is likely to permit the real, spontaneous shudders to come at any turn of the narrative.

Acting a Part

Often in order to help your client break through the patterns which are keeping her from talking about that which she needs to talk about, or from discharging painful emotion that she needs to discharge, you will play a kind of dramatic role.

You will act like, or sometimes unlike, the characters who were associated with the tensions which she is trying to get rid of. This character-playing will be always understood to be sheer pretense and will never obscure your basic role of being sincerely concerned, warmly interested and friendly.

Repeatedly Check for Identifications

When a client talks about and shows tension on people, you as counselor need always to check for the earlier person with whom identification has been made.

Tension from a father often becomes transferred to a husband. By working over these identifications with all the techniques at your disposal, the tension on the identified characters will be lessened. Also, very important, they will become separated from each other and thus each be much easier to re-evaluate on. The husband who no longer is identified with the father becomes someone off whom the tensions can be discharged much more easily than before the identification was broken.

Counselor, Too

This need to ferret out, discharge and re-evaluate on identifications of one person with another applies with special force to the counselor. In the beginning of work with any client, you should check, "Whom do I remind you of," and try to get the client to express his spontaneous thoughts on this, even if he doubts on the awareness level that such resemblance exists. It does not matter if the person with whom you become identified is positive or negative in his role in the person's past. Tensions attaching to him will tend to become tied to you and create great difficulties in the counseling relationship.

"Whom do I remind you of?" "How am I like him?" "How else am I like him?" "How else am I like him?" etc. "How am I different from him?" "How did you feel toward him?" Here again, even if the response is, "Oh fine, I had complete trust and confidence in that person," this, too, needs to be expressed.

If you as counselor become identified with Uncle Pete from the client's past who was mean and cruel and wasn't understanding, then of course it is obvious that the client attaching these characteristics to you will find it very difficult to work well with you. But it is equally true that if the client identifies you with Uncle Henry, who was kind and good and understanding and always gave him candy whenever he visited, there can be a difficulty, too. Because unless the identification is brought out, discussed and counseled on, a good session with you will nevertheless leave the client feeling frustrated and disappointed in you without knowing why. The reason being (below awareness) that you failed to really be Uncle Henry and let him leave the session without a bag of candy or some similar gift.

Persisting with Discharge

Beginning counselors are usually amazed and sometimes appalled at how persistently the discharge needs to be maintained. For the client's sake, everything depends on staying with discharge until all the tension is released, but the creeping restimulation of the counselor is likely to make anything else about the client's case seem more interesting and important. The counselor has to remember that the client, too, is compulsively eager to get away from the discharge and leave part of it still stored, so that *only the counselor can be depended on to furnish the persistence necessary.*

Clients who speak of having "cried for days" before counseling will, after a two-hour continuous discharge of tears, usually estimate the session as more crying than they had done in all their life previously.

GOALS OF THE COUNSELOR

The only workable goal for a counselor to have with a client is the one of freeing the client from the aberration. The only effective means of doing this is the discharge of painful emotion or pain tensions and the re-evaluation by the client *herself* of the experience involved.

Other reactive goals will tend to interpose themselves in the counselor's way largely as a result of restimulation. The off-beam character of these are often obvious when they show up as "trying to please the client," "trying to make the client comfortable," "having a good visit," "showing the client who's boss," and so on.

Others are more insidious because of widespread misconceptions in our culture. "Finding out what's wrong with the client," "getting to the bottom of what makes her that way," "finding out what she's really trying to hide," "understanding him," "getting some experience in counseling," etc., may sound like acceptable goals for a counselor, but they are as wrong and unworkable as the others.

The only workable goal for a counselor is the freeing of the client from aberration through discharge and re-evaluation.

COUNSELING FIRST-AID ON INJURIES

Physical tensions and pains (as distinct from emotional) will become available for discharge *only* after most of the painful emotion surrounding them have been released.

There is a kind of exception to this, however, in the case of the new physical injury which has just occurred. Where a person has just been hurt physically, (anything from a bumped knee to a serious operation), there appears to be a time lag, before the pain and the physical tension of the injury becomes so stored away and surrounded by painful emotion as to be unavailable. In this interval, roughly the interval when the injury is still "hurting," it is possible to discharge and release the physical pain and tension *immediately* by approaching it directly.

This is done by experiencing the hurt, the pain, the physical tension as thoroughly as possible over and over again while reviewing the actual occurrence of the injury. The person can even do this quite well by her or himself, but of course a second person, a counselor, makes it easier to be thorough.

By repetitively going over the injury and "making the hurt *hurt*" and by experiencing the pain or tension intensely over and over again, the pain and the physical distress will disappear or seem to become erased. Usually, some emotional tensions will come off in the familiar laughter, tears, trembling, etc., as the pain is gone over. But the pain will also dissipate, usually with stretching and yawns coming in the last stages. A very few minutes counseling will suffice for a small injury (or a very few hours for even a grievous injury) to undo the stored up physical pain and shock.

The effects of this kind of counseling first-aid appear almost magical. Pain is relieved permanently. The person does not suffer from the injury so long as it is protected from fresh assaults, bumps, bruises, etc. Healing is very rapid, appearing to match the healing rate which we observe in very young children.

Burns and Folklore

Often people have acquired patterns of pain suppression which make it hard for them to actually experience and fully recover from their recent injuries. Sometimes incidental measures can be taken to assist them.

A sunburn, for example, can be worked on with a very warm tub of water. It becomes very easy to experience the pain of the sunburn in full measure for a few minutes. The pain will then soon lift and the distress of the sunburn will be gone — for good.

The old wives' remedy of "flame draws fire" procedure for burn injuries is also workable. Placing a new burn injury near a hot object or near a flame makes it hurt more intensely. If a person finds it difficult to actually experience the pain of a burn, placing it near a heater or hot object will cause the pain to be experienced very vividly for a short period and then be gone, gone for good. The burn will then heal rapidly if protected from fresh injury.

ADVANCED COUNSELING

Your elementary skills in counseling will keep you busy for a long time. There is no limit to what you can accomplish with them provided you see that you yourself have adequate counseling.

All around you are people whom you can help to live better and more intelligently. Even the members of your own family (whose cases seem so confusing because of the mutual restimulation) can be assisted directly (and more easily by an exchange with your Co-Counselor of work with each other's families).

More advanced counseling knowledge will be something you will wish to have in time for the more rapid resolution of later stages in your own case. Doing a good job of Co-Counseling with your elementary techniques will lead you to this naturally and, in the process, transform your life.

*   *   *

NO SOCIALIZING*

Co-Counseling students and Co-Counselors are requested and expected to refrain from establishing any relationship, except that of Co-Counselor, with the students and clients whom they meet in Re-evaluation Counseling.

It is an inherent requirement of Re-evaluation Counseling that students and clients shall refrain from setting up other relationships than that of Co-Counseling with students and clients whom they meet in Re-evaluation Counseling.

Attempts to establish any other relationship — social, romantic, etc. — will not only be in violation of one's responsibility, but will also be unsuccessful and certain in the very nature of the situation to lead to difficulties.

Successful Co-Counseling is quite likely to make one (or both) of the counselors feel that they have at last discovered the ideal person to have a friendship with, a social relationship. It can even happen that the Co-Counselor will appear as the long-sought "girl (or boy) of my dreams." Such feelings will occur and no amount of discussion will prevent them. The fact

---

* The no socializing section of this *Manual* was printed on blue paper in early editions, to call it to the attention of the students. This was the origin of the term "blue pages" which is today a by-word throughout the Re-evaluation Counseling Communities.

is, such feelings can be a very positive occurrence BUT they do *not* have to be acted upon, *nor should they be.* The Co-Counselor or fellow student is to remain and be treated as a Co-Counselor or fellow student, no matter how the student "feels" about them. To do otherwise will simply not work.

The reason for this is that an unaware assumption is always made that the subject of one's socializing, dating, or romantic attitude will basically remain a counselor to one and remain responsible for one in this new relationship. This will be impossible for him or her, of course, if they respond in a socializing or romantic way.

Essentially, the person who does this is seeking a way to escape the discomfort of discharging and getting rid of the reactive material which has prevented him from making friends by substituting a Co-Counselor for the friends he needs to make in the outside world. He is avoiding solving his difficulties that are interfering with successful loving relationships by casting the Co-Counselor in the role of a beloved who will also remain (he unawarely assumes) perfectly permissive even to distresses.

These feelings will not work if acted upon outside of Co-Counseling. The student client may, in a session, tell his Co-Counselor repeatedly "you are my friend," "I have a friend," "you feel friendly to me," and discharge greatly and make fine progress. If he carries this outside the counseling session and bundles up himself or family and goes to pay a social call upon his Co-Counselor, he will soon find that his patterns have fouled up the friendly relationship he intended to have, and spoiled the Co-Counseling relationship as well.

If student Co-Counselors attempt to date or to be romantic, they will very soon have a mess on their hands and their Co-Counseling relationship will be ruined. If they hold their feelings to the Co-Counseling session and verbalize the "I love you's" repeatedly there, it can well bring hours of shaking, tears, laughter and other good results. The end result will be that the client will like his counselor but will be free from any dependent or romantic attachment.

It is always difficult for elementary students who feel the pull of these escapes to conceive that the rule is realistic. Perhaps it is sufficient to say that several score people have by now violated this rule, followed their feelings rather than logical responsibility, and not one good social or romantic relationship has come out of it. A few have been lost to Co-Counseling progress over this. Most, of course, have spotted the bad results and drawn back to follow workable procedures.

This is an inherent requirement for successful participation in a Co-Counseling class or group that the Co-Counselor remains just that — a Co-Counselor.

There are people who come to Re-evaluation Counseling with other relationships already established — married couples, engaged couples, friends, lovers. These already-established relationships can, of course, be maintained and, in general, will be improved with the addition of a Co-Counseling relationship. It is where the acquaintance is first made in the counseling atmosphere that this rule applies.

THE ART OF BEING A CLIENT

This *Manual* is written for the Co-Counselor in his/her role as counselor and properly so. All of us retain spontaneous motivations toward being clients, however much these motivations may seem obscured by inhibiting patterns. It is in becoming an effective counselor that we all need detailed guidance and encouragement in overcoming the conditioning against discharge and against assisting discharge which our culture has placed upon us.

Nevertheless, most of the rewards of Co-Counseling come to us as clients. Our success as clients, that is, in discharging and re-evaluating our own distresses, is the primary factor in the long-range success we have as counselors. Skill in functioning as a client is of great importance. The following guidelines, extracted from many experiences by many people in being clients, will be helpful.

First, *take and keep responsibility for one's self as a client.* It is marvelous to feel the responsibility of one's counselor standing by when one is in the throes of heavy discharge; but in between times it is best to remember to think about and plan for one's own progress as a client. One will have much better sessions if one comes to them with an idea in mind of what one wants to work on, and allows even the most skilled counselor to fill his/her proper role as one's helper rather than having to try to plan for the client.

Second, one should act like a client during sessions and *only* during sessions. One will certainly have many informal, short or telephone sessions as well as one's formal ones, but one should try to be sure that the other person is ready and willing to be counselor before one "let's go" with one's distresses. To do otherwise is not only unfair to and an imposition on one's counselors, but it will not work really well for the client over the long haul.

Third, lovingly *care for and nurture one's counselors.* A person who can counsel one well is a treasure, to be treated with courtesy and consideration, to be appreciated openly and well, to be given one's best counseling back when the roles are reversed (and, if one is not yet able to counsel him or her equally well, to be tendered baby-sitting, lawn-mowing, floor-scrubbing, or other valuable considerations so that the relationship remains fair and mutually self-respecting).

Fourth, *one should act during and between sessions so that any observers will be drawn to the use of Re-evaluation Counseling* by the example of how responsibly one frees one's self from one's distresses, rather than be repelled by the carelessness with which one exhibits and dramatizes one's material.

To inflict on other people in the environment examples of how loudly or daringly one can yell, scream, curse or repeat words forbidden in childhood is exhibitionism and the rehearsal of a distress pattern and *is not discharge nor responsible counseling.*

A client will sometimes need to yell or scream in order to get discharge started, but the yelling or screaming is not itself discharge, and can be done into a pillow or out of earshot of others when it is necessary.

Wrecking furniture or counseling rooms or other destructive violence is not discharge but is the unhelpful rehearsal of a pattern. Violent movement is necessary for some kinds of discharge, but this is easily achieved by jumping up and down violently on a firm floor, with no harm to anything nor upset to the neighbors.

Warmth and closeness grow naturally between Co-Counselors and between members of Co-Counseling groups or Co-Counseling Communities and is to be treasured and enjoyed, but this is a private matter. To embarrassedly or defensively engage in embraces in situations where such embraces will not be understood or to blindly try to impose such closeness on others, who, through no fault of theirs, do not or cannot understand, is again exhibitionism, not counseling.

All persons not yet in the Re-evaluation Counseling Community must be treated awarely and with respect, must be communicated with on the basis of *where they are, not* on the basis of how *we* feel, or where we wish they were.

A Co-Counselor once summed this up by saying, "We just mustn't wipe our stuff on other people or think that will help us get rid of it."

Co-Counselors must endeavor, like Caesar's wife, to be above reproach in their relations with all other people. And because we are Co-Counselors, always growing and gaining, this will turn out to be not so difficult as it might seem.

— Harvey Jackins
August 1971

MY GOALS

	NEXT WEEK	NEXT MONTH	IN A YEAR	FOR 5 YEARS	FOR 20 YEARS	FOR ALWAYS
FOR ME						
FOR MY FAMILY						
FOR MY ALLIES						
FOR HUMANKIND						
FOR ALL LIVING THINGS						
FOR THE UNIVERSE						

THE KEY CONCEPTS AND INSIGHTS OF RE-EVALUATION COUNSELING TO DATE

— Harvey Jackins

This is a summary of a report to the 1981 World Conference published in ***The Reclaiming of Power****.*

Our experience indicates that we must wage at least three struggles at the same time, that every RC meeting needs to contain at least three elements. One is the review of the theory which we already know, but which continually becomes occluded by restimulation. Two is the keeping up-to-date with the emerging theory. Three is the actual participation in the re-emergence process.

This morning I am going to list and comment on the basic RC concepts which we have absorbed and integrated partially but the forgetting of which seems to be behind almost every serious difficulty that our Community experiences.

The first insight is not limited to RC. We share it in common with all sciences and with all useful philosophies. This is the assumption or realization that **an objective universe exists.** We assume that it would exist or does exist independently of our observation of it, at least on the macroscopic level, at least on the level of large bodies and more-than-nuclear distances. There is some question whether our observation of it does not become an integral part of it on the level of very, very small distances and sub-atomic relationships, but on the level of relationships with which we ordinarily deal, our assumption is that the universe exists independently of our thinking about it.

Now, to the particular insights of RC. The first is that **the distress experience is the source of and the explanation for human irrationality.** Most of us have integrated this, but we sometimes don't act as if we had. We still blame and reproach people. This is the key insight into the (up-until-now, and outside of RC) unsolved problem of human irrationality that threatens every other phase of human existence.

The recorded distress experience is the sole source of human irrationality. The only thing wrong with people is the result of mistreatment. (I am not saying deliberate mistreatment, because most of it is not.)

The second is that the process which we call discharge, the complex process or set of processes dependably characterized by tears; trembling; yawning; many kinds of laughter; live, righteous storming; interested, non-repetitive talk (or in some cases, thinking enhanced by the expectation of eventual talk, which is the case with "rapid review"); this set of processes that we familiarly refer to as **"discharge," is the recovery process from irrationality, from distress.** Our great respect for discharge is justified. We act in many counseling circumstances as if discharge were our goal. We even tell students in fundamentals classes that "all you are after is discharge," which is not quite true and has to be corrected in later classes by reminding the students that the real goal is re-emergence, not discharge. Because discharge has been so inhibited and the inhibitions on it are a principal obstacle to re-emergence, we often treat discharge as if it were the principal goal of our Co-Counseling activity.

Third is the concept, the understanding, that **re-evaluation occurs spontaneously following discharge.** All the notions that still circulate in the society and in the educational systems—that a counselor or teacher must replace the "bad" ideas with "good" ideas—are false. Only a person's own thinking is good enough to guide that person, and that thinking takes place spontaneously following discharge. This does not mean that we don't share experiences and information. It doesn't mean that we don't find inspiration in each other's ideas, but it does mean that the person's own thinking is the crux of the matter and that thinking occurs spontaneously. Our assistance to each other is not in "helping each other think," even though we use that phrase carelessly sometimes. Our assistance to each other is in helping each other discharge so that we can each think for ourselves.

Four: **Any distress can be completely discharged.** This real possibility of the complete discharge of any distress is little realized and less practiced in our Communities until now. It was demonstrated many times in the early days of RC, in Seattle, when we followed one-way clients for a long time and made it a practice with many of them to clean up distress completely. The possibility of the complete discharge of distress is very important even though it has been neglected in the "half-hour each way" sessions which dominated Co-Counseling in the early years of the Communities.

Following from this, and right alongside of it, is the complete recoverability of the human capacity which the distress has occluded. **One's occluded abilities and capacities can be completely recovered.**

Next is **the fundamental difference between the pattern and the person.** They are two separate entities even though one is sitting at the back of the other's head and often manipulating its voice, even though one follows the other around and appears to speak for it. There is a fundamental distinction between the human being and the distress pattern. They are two completely separate kinds of entities. I doubt if there is any confusion that is more widespread or one that creates more difficulty in the wide-world activities of human beings than just exactly this, confusing the pattern with the person and the person with the pattern. We slip into this confusion often. Whenever we argue with distress, we have slipped into this. Whenever we blame or reproach the person, we have slipped into this. It is not yet so well understood or so well remembered that we do not need to repeat it again and again. The distress pattern is of a completely different character than the human being.

Next is the integral, wholesome goodness of the human being. In this insight we reject thousands of years of cultural mistakes and hundreds and hundreds of religions and theories which assume, for understandable reasons, that the human being is a mixture of good and evil. We reject this. It is crucial and important that **the human being, as a human being, is integral, is wholesome, is good.** The patterns may be of great variety, including some pseudo-survival varieties, but the human being, as distinct from the pattern, is one-piece, is consistent, is wholesome, is good. The human being, as a human being, distinct from the distress patterns which parasite on it and infest it, is completely "upward trend."

The next important concept is our rejection of any cultural standards of "normality," our refusal to accept any cultural definitions of what is a fully-functioning person. We are not opposed to any temporary goals for improvement, but we refuse to accept any of the present limits which cultures place upon the flowering of human beings. We insist that the boldest and freest definition of a human being is misleading, that the capacity of a human being is limitless and cannot be defined. We haven't any notion of what any real limits for a human being might be. Any goal that we set, once attained, immediately projects a further, loftier goal. **We refuse to accept any cultural definition of normality or goodness that puts limits on the human being.**

Feelings are not a reliable guide to action. This seems familiar to most of us by now, doesn't it? We remember it, we tell it to other people, we even act on it ourselves part of the time; but isn't it hard to remember all the time? Isn't this a continual struggle that we wage, to not act on our feelings, no matter how righteous they sometimes seem?

Only logic is a reliable guide to action. If we have good feelings, fine, enjoy them, but do not act on them. If we have terrible feelings, contradict them and discharge them, but do not act on them. Act on logic and logic alone (or the best approximation of logic that we can make in sometimes confusing conditions).

Logic is the way the human mind works in the absence of distress. It has also been defined in workable, useful ways by logicians starting with Aristotle. Aristotle and his successors and, more recently, Goedel and Church and a number of other people, have been able to get outside the confusion and distress and state the rules of logic very concisely and very accurately. One of these rules is that a statement cannot be true and untrue at the same time in the same situation. Another is that if statement A means that statement B is true, and statement B means that statement C is true, then statement A means that statement C is true. Others are a little more complicated.

Patterns are addictive in their actions. Patterns tend to force their victim through a re-enactment of the original hurt that caused the pattern. It is an important insight that a pattern tends to force its victim through a repetition, as far as possible, of the original hurt. What are called addictions in ordinary usage are the effects of patterns. Patterns are addictive in the sense that yielding to the compelling feelings embodied in patterns is the necessary and sufficient explanation of addiction. Understanding this opens the way to freeing people from addictions.

A pattern tends always to force its victim through as close a repetition as possible of the original hurt experience. What are ordinarily called addictions, i.e., addictions to poisonous chemical substances, operate on exactly this basis. Patterns are addictive in themselves. Chemical addictions operate only through patterns. With these insights, addictions can be removed and the victim can become free from them by applying what we know about counseling.

(The withdrawal period for an addict coming off a chemical addiction is described in the usual literature as a terrible experience. Such people are locked up in steel cells alone because nobody "can stand to be around them" as they go through withdrawal. This is exactly wrong. Withdrawal is just the thawing out from numbness of the feelings of hurt of the original poisoning. The feeling is felt as it thaws out, and discharge accompanies it. The withdrawal procedure can be greatly expedited by giving counseling attention to the person. D.T.'s, [delirium tremens], the wild clamoring and the wild shaking traditional to alcoholics sobering up, is exactly discharge taking place. It can be greatly accelerated and expedited and completed by giving counseling attention to the person doing it.)

Complete self-appreciation is possible. It is justified by reality, and attempting it is very productive. **Complete self-appreciation is a reasonable and useful goal.** Realizing this was one of the great turning points in the practice of Re-evaluation Counseling. Complete self-appreciation, no reservations.

This next crucial insight is the content of the first scroll we ever produced. It continues to out-sell all the others. What it says is, **"Every single human being at every moment of the past, if the entire situation is taken into account, has always done the very best he or she could do and so deserves neither blame nor reproach from anyone, including self. This, in particular, is true of you."** It is still just as fresh as it ever was, isn't it? It is one of our key insights, often forgotten temporarily but returned to, over and over.

Our past is determined. Our future is free choice. Just incidentally, this resolves one of the great philosophical dilemmas that had persisted for thousands of years—the controversy between determinism and free will. It resolves when you run the line of present time between the past and the future. The two halves of the dilemma fall open and there is no longer any contradiction.

The insight arose out of our practical work, and it has great practical significance. As counselors, we can clearly, without hesitation, throw all our influence to contradict the client's regrets and self-reproaches about the past or his or her powerlessness or apathy about the future.

The past is determined. Waste no regrets. Waste no remorse. You cannot bring father back to life by wishing you had told him to take the train instead of the plane. You can only say your goodbye to him and shed your tears thoroughly. But, on the other hand, "I never could" doesn't mean "I can't." The future is free.

How can you be a successful counselor and always help your client achieve discharge? **Any distress discharges when it is contradicted sufficiently.**

We can now state a four-step rule for successful counseling. Applying it may stretch you a little bit occasionally, but it is a dependable rule. Step zero, review the counselor's goal as seeing to it that the client re-emerges decisively, remembering that the client is inherently a person of great intelligence, value, decisiveness, and power as well as needing assistance with emergence from distress, and, in particular, noticing and remembering where this particular client is capable, treasurable, and already functioning, or close to functioning, elegantly and well. Step one, pay enough attention to the client to see clearly what his or her distresses are. This includes, of course, asking him or her questions and listening to him or her, as well as observing him or her. Step two is to think; to think of all possible ways those distresses can be contradicted. Step three is to contradict them sufficiently. If you do these four things, discharge will always come.

The most common mistake that we make in our counseling is that we contradict the distress a little bit and if we don't get discharge, we conclude we are on the wrong track. We stop short. We fail to put our confidence into the situation. The words "enough" or "sufficiently" are important here.

There is no rational conflict of interest between human beings. Contrary to almost everything you have been told, contrary to the appearances of much of what you see going on in this society, this insight breaks through to reality. There is no rational conflict of interest between any human beings.

There is an ancient story: While still alive, a man is taken to visit Hell and then Heaven as a special dispensation to guide him on his behavior. When he comes to Hell, he hears behind closed doors great wailing and reproaching and gnashing of teeth. When the doors open, the condemned souls are sitting at tables where a great feast is spread. It is lovely food, but the condemned souls are starving. Out of their hands grow long spoons and forks, so long that they cannot reach their mouths with them, and they are starving in the midst of plenty, unable to reach the food, in despair, suffering terribly. The visitor is then taken to Heaven, to an identical building. Happy sounds are coming from the closed doors. There are murmurs of laughter, of joy. When the doors open, the blessed souls are sitting at tables spread with a succulent feast. Out of their arms also grow spoons and forks too long to reach their mouths, but the blessed souls are contentedly feeding each other.

There is no rational conflict of interest between human beings. This is a very important touchstone to refer to since most of people's effort, most of people's energy, most of people's time is enlisted by the irrational, oppressive society in irrational conflicts.

A great part of the effort of wide-world liberation forces gets turned to mass mailings, to billboards, to thundering from pulpits, to leafletting, to mass meetings. These are not generally effective. **For important ideas, one-to-one communication is necessary.**

It is always possible for any individual to take the initiative in any situation. Because of the early conditioning to be helpless and powerless, this has been a difficult concept to comprehend. Sometimes the initiative might simply be to yell for help although one has been conditioned not to do that. This idea is very close to the freedom to choose one's viewpoint, which is one of our more recent insights, but this one has been with us some time. It is part of the Postulates. **In any situation, it is always possible for an individual to take the initiative and to take charge of the situation by doing so.**

The next concept is that **complete responsibility is the natural attitude of each human being.** The almost universal helpless, irresponsible, hopeless, dragged out, bewildered attitudes are all conditioning, all stuck on by hurts. The attitude of complete responsibility was the inherent one.

Love is the way people naturally feel about each other. Our loving attitude to others is waiting there to be uncovered as the distress is removed. It is not something to be beaten into a child with punishment. It is not something to be attained by the restimulation of sexual feelings. It is the way people naturally feel about each other.

Goals can be awarely chosen at all levels of responsibility and future time. There is a goals chart in the back of our *Fundamentals Manual*. We drew it up about twenty-eight years ago. When a teacher focuses attention on the importance of this, students begin to clarify whole areas of their lives.

One can set one's own goals. It is possible. One does not have to have goals set for one by anyone else. This is itself a revolutionary concept. One can set goals for all of the different concentric spheres of one's responsibility. One can set goals for oneself. One can set goals to achieve in relation to one's close intimate loved ones, for one's extended family, for one's various groups, for one's city, county, state, nation, province, for one's continent, for one's species, for the world of living things, and for the universe as a whole. Not only can one set goals at all these levels, but setting them at all levels greatly reinforces the power of the goals. Every level of goals becomes more workable if integrated with all other levels.

One can also set goals at all levels of time. In fact, one needs to set goals for all levels of time. One needs to plan at least what one will accomplish today, this week, this month, this year, and in ten years. One needs a clear picture of what one wants to do before one climbs the ladder to the space ship to colonize the next planet. To set these goals for all these times and at all these levels and integrate them makes immediate goals much more easily achievable. Our practical experience is that if a person sets only an immediate goal, she or he will mill around indefinitely and discharge on that goal without achieving it, but that if a farther goal is set, he or she will discharge while achieving the immediate one and will tackle the next one.

An upward trend exists in the universe counter to the entropy trend, but compatible with it. Our position in the universe is on the rising point, the advanced point of the upward trend. The upward trend exists everywhere. I have been thinking lately about the great adventure stories that have thrilled generations of people. Almost always the climax of the story is at a point when the hero or heroine has done his or her best, has been confused and bewildered, but has struggled onward. Then the upward trend appears from out of its occlusion. The upward trend appears and buoys up the hero's or heroine's efforts, and triumph takes place. No wonder these stories thrilled us. The writer intuitively reached for this great insight.

Leadership functions must be performed if a group is to function well. An operating leaderless group is a fiction. A leaderless, collapsing group is, of course, common. At least one person must think about the group as a whole rather than just her or his role in it. This is the key leadership function. **The leadership functions must be filled for any group to operate well.**

We are getting past one-person leadership. When we said "at least one person must think about the group as a whole," and we put key responsibility on the Area Reference Person, it sometimes came to be distorted in practice to mean only one person was encouraged to think of the group as a whole. We are learning to push ahead the realization that every person in a group can share the general leadership function of thinking about the group as a whole and can handle the specific leadership tasks by a division of responsibility.

It is possible for a rational group discussion to take place. It astounds some of our wide-world friends when they first run into the simple concepts of an RC topic group or discussion group. They are simple concepts, but they work well if you take them into the wide world. "No person speaks twice before everyone speaks once." "No one speaks four times before everyone speaks twice." "Discussions shall involve issues but not personalities." "Everyone shall be listened to with respect." "A summary of the important things said in a subgroup shall be prepared for the larger group, oral and/or written." Just these simple guidelines have unleashed a tremendous flood of excellent thinking of which we have been able to capture just a portion in our journals.

Individual thinking is greatly enhanced by attentive, non-responsive listening. One of the brightest jewels in our crown of innovations is the Think and Listen Group where each person has the opportunity to be listened to with attention, and no response or comment on any other speaker's thoughts is permitted. There is no assignment of topic. To have such an experience tremendously enhances a person's thinking and gives one a clear view of how much our thinking and our speaking are usually inhibited by fear of the response of the person listening. When we set up a real Think and Listen Group, and our thinking is protected by this crystal chalice of non-intervention, our minds flower and brilliant thoughts come forth. Think and Listens have often been misrepresented by calling groups by this name in which people take turns speaking on a common or assigned topic; Think and Listens are not like this at all.

It is possible to deliberately create oases of safety for thinking, for discharge, and for re-evaluation. In our sessions we have certain agreements that are supposed to be followed. This is true also in our topic groups, in our Think and Listens, in our classes, in our Communities, in our workshops. When these agreements are followed, it becomes possible to achieve things because of the safety that we cannot achieve under other circumstances. Violation of these agreements makes progress difficult and leads to some disappointing situations. Awarely facing and keeping these agreements enhance our functioning greatly.

What is so wonderful about a session? The counselor and client are agreed on how each is to behave. If the counselor gives her or his opinion, or reproaches the client, or allows an upset look on her or his face when the client is trying to get at some sticky material, the safety is destroyed. You know what happens in a workshop when someone is laboriously trying to say something important about his or her oppression and somebody from the oppressor group's guilt flames and he or she gets up and interrupts and "corrects" the speaker. The safety is gone.

Those of you who were at Liberation I and II remember the great turning point in that long afternoon when no whites were allowed to speak until all people of color had spoken as much as they wanted to. That made the difference. The workshop got safer and safer and safer, and the people of color thought better and spoke more clearly, and our liberation work was splendidly launched. We create atmospheres of safety.

I have tried to think of analogies. The best one I have thought of so far is of those Middle Ages cultures where everybody went around in armor. What do we create in the session, in the support group, in the class, in the workshop, in the Community? We create an environment where it is possible to risk taking off your armor so you can wash your underwear. If you have to wear your armor, it is pretty hard to wash your underwear. In a good session, a good workshop, a good support group, where the rules are not forgotten for anybody, we can flourish.

Every once in a while at a teachers' and leaders' workshop, everything falls together and people take huge strides forward. There are other times when people are not that responsible. Sometimes we still accomplish something, but we accomplish it on bruised, scraped knees and with gritted teeth. Bring this concept up into awareness, that our RC environments, wherever we can set them up, are basically oases of safety, and the more deliberately and carefully we can create them, the cleaner our underwear will be. Also, we'll be able to get by with lighter-weight armor for the times in between because we will be so confident. Our oases can grow bigger. Everyone can take the safety of a workshop home and extend it to his or her family and neighborhood.

Oppression exists universally in present societies. Every person in our societies is locked into both oppressed and oppressor roles. I sometimes get the impression that we have gotten used to this concept very quickly. Then I hear discussions that completely ignore it and get way off track as a result. Out in the wide world this is still almost unknown and unfaced—this realization that everyone in our societies has been forced into operating within both oppressor and oppressed roles.

Oppression only operates, and can only operate, through distress patterns. This, again, is one of the most powerful insights about oppression. It has been useful to us but is desperately needed by oppression fighters and liberation movements in the wide world. It is useful, in part, because otherwise the disheartening appearance of human beings, who we assume are good and wholesome, acting in such oppressive, unwholesome ways tends to destroy our morale and blight our spirit over and over again. No person would ever agree to or submit to being oppressed unless a pattern of oppression had first been installed, in the first place by young people's oppression in his or her early childhood. The oppression of young people, and the installation of patterns of oppression through the oppression of young people, is the foundation that allows other oppressions to be installed.

Only the distress patterns left by the oppression of young people allow other oppressions to be accepted. Only the installation of oppressed patterns makes it possible to force a person to continue to function as oppressed. **No one would agree to or submit to being oppressed for more than an instant except for the installation of distress patterns.** A victim of oppressive forces might bide his or her time and keep a submissive facial expression while the gun was pointed at him or her, but the oppressor would be overthrown very quickly if the distress patterns of being oppressed were not internalized to enforce the person.

More than that, no person would agree to function as an oppressor for an instant if the patterns of oppression had not first been installed (by that person being oppressed) and the person then manipulated into the oppressor role in the pattern. **The oppressor, the person who functions as an oppressor, has always first been oppressed and then manipulated into the other end of the oppression pattern.** The great breakthrough insight here came from England at an Arundel workshop when the first "born to rule" caucus met. About six people were hanging onto each other and shaking wildly as several of their number reported on what it was like to be ruling class in England. I remember one describing the extra oppression of preparation for being "presented to the Queen." Others told of how they were taken from their parents at an early age and sent to special schools called "public schools" and there systematically tortured and degraded in the most inhumane ways. They were then manipulated in later years into the other end of the pattern, forced to give the same vicious treatment to the younger boys in preparation for their "ruling" role.

This realization, this principle, is at first met with indignation by victims of oppression. "You're trying to tell me that those were innocent humans, those people who tortured and shot, and gouged out my family's eyes? You are going to tell me that Hitler was a human being?" Yes. It is of great support to us to realize that the most viciously functioning person in the world was a human being underneath the distress and functioned so viciously only because of the distress. This empowers us and emboldens us to seek allies much more widely, to keep up our own morale and our strength. We have a scroll saying that, "If a distress pattern attacks you (and nothing else ever does), help is always close at hand. This is the human being locked inside the distress pattern, the pattern's victim and your best ally, who can be reached in ways that we are learning to do."

The person who functions as an oppressor does so always and only because he or she has first been oppressed, and the pattern of oppression thus installed, and has then been manipulated into the other end of the pattern in order to function as an oppressor. **If we can help the person acting out an oppressor role in a pattern to discharge that pattern, or manipulate the person out of it, that person will gladly cease functioning as an oppressor and will become an ally.**

Oppression can be and is internalized. The realization that oppression is usually internalized, if we can communicate it widely enough, will make a great difference in our work. If we can reach the liberation forces of the world with our understanding of internalized oppression, we will redouble their strength several times. People are eager and willing to understand this.

Most damage done by oppression is done by its internalized form. To realize this is of importance in eliminating oppression, in discharging oppression patterns. The blows from outside came early, they will still come occasionally, they come viciously sometimes when the struggle is joined; but almost all the damage done by oppression is done by its internalized persistence, by the self-invalidation, self-attack, attacks upon each other by the members of the oppressed group and by the fierce attacks and competition between different oppressed groups that otherwise would be, and can become, each other's supportive allies.

A classical example, spotted by sociologists long ago, is the game, "The Dozens," played by young U.S. black men, in which the object is to remain "cool" and "calm" while insulting each other and degrading each other in the most vicious possible ways. The game continues on and on. Each new generation of young black men is expected to participate in this cruel, cruel invalidation procedure. It has been traced to its origins in the necessity for black mothers under slavery to humiliate their male children into submissiveness in order that they could remain alive. Under slavery, if male black children showed any trace of spirit or rebellion, this so severely frightened the slave owner that they were subject to instant execution. Black mothers deliberately kept their black sons alive by humiliating them and degrading them and forcing them into submissive patterns of behavior in which they were expected to endure without resistance. This did keep them alive. The tactic was successful, but the internalizing of the oppression has carried on generation after generation to this day (with some reinforcement, of course, from new oppression) with the persistence and contagion which we have recognized that patterns can have.

The person outside a particular oppression can be powerfully effective against the internalized form of the oppression. Contrary to what seems to be the reality (and, of course, is actually our fears), when black people invalidate each other, compete with each other, pool their discouragement and hopelessness, and the white person draws back and doesn't dare say anything about black oppression (because the white person is "of course not an expert and doesn't want to intrude and make a fool of himself or herself"), contrary to that is the reality that an aware white person in a group of black people can be decisively effective in interrupting the internalized oppression simply by seeing the viciousness of it and speaking clearly from the outside. At the first Latino workshop the Chicana women were speaking out of their internalized oppression about how ugly they felt and how they longed for long, blonde, straight hair all the time they were growing up. I felt sincerely indignant because these were beautiful women, all of them, without exception, and I spoke from my heart and said, "How can you talk that way? You are the most beautiful women in the world." At first they felt that I was being sarcastic and wanted to fight with me, but then they heard that I meant it, and heavy discharge took place, just enormous discharge on this material. Up to that point they could only be sarcastic with each other. The person outside the oppression can be very effective against the internalized oppression.

This is nearly an exact analog of the intelligence of the counselor speaking from outside the individual distress pattern. If the counselor sees the client's distress as it is going on, and acts to contradict it, what a great lift it gives one, as client. How heavily we discharge! It is almost an exact analog of this, that the person outside the oppression can contradict the internalized oppression effectively.

For some time we men stood around bewildered and timid and fumble-footed while we watched the struggle of women to liberate themselves. Just now we are beginning to find out that we don't have to stand back, ashamed of our sexism and apologizing for it forever. We can move in and be of great assistance to the emergence of women from the internalized oppression.

Liberation from oppression requires a three-point program: one, a clear liberation policy; two, unity of the group around that policy; and three, the winning of allies. The members of the oppressed group should participate in the working out of the policy. Working out the policy can help to achieve unity among the oppressed group. You will achieve the policy and the unity at the same time. The third step is the winning of allies. This has been known intuitively (outside of RC) in a very few quarters, but almost all liberation movements have neglected it, almost entirely. Almost all the liberation activities of the past have floundered and wasted their resources for lack of that third action, the winning of allies.

People need separate discussions within each particular liberation group before they can hope to communicate well to, or unite with, the other groups. Whenever this principle has been applied, it has been very powerful. Where it has not been applied, such as in the drift into having an oppressed group and its allies in the same mixed support group or workshop, we have inevitably developed difficulties that take time and trouble to sort out. Each group must caucus separately first in spite of their fears of segregation and their eager desire for unity. They must have a time to get themselves together in the safety of their similarities, their commonalities, or their homogeneity. People having the same backgrounds need to first discuss and agree on what they want the other groups to hear from them. Once that is accomplished, they can come together and listen to each other with respect, and achieve the real unity that they would otherwise seek too quickly or too simplistically.

This principle has been forgotten over and over. Working-class support groups, for example, have started enthusiastically and then many times tended to wither because of the considerable differences in backgrounds among the twenty or thirty people that enthusiastically come out at first. They have one or two good meetings and then, unsafety. Individual members complain bitterly about "the things they had to listen to." The underlying unity is obscured by the differences.

Recently, we had the first workshop restricted just to industrial workers, and it was so fine and free. Everyone there knew what everyone else was talking about. Discussions quickly came to agreement. It was delightfully different from past workshops. Yet in the future when we have a workshop where the industrial workers who have been working separately come together with the medical workers who have been working separately and the clerical workers who have been working separately, we have enough experience to say confidently that the different groups will understand each other and come to a fine unity. This principle of the necessity of preliminary separations whenever there are differences—in order to communicate well towards a wider unity later—deserves to be dusted off and proclaimed over and over again.

Each particular oppression has certain features in common with all other oppressions. Every oppression, for example, includes a lack of respect for members of the oppressed group. There are many other such elements which are common to every oppression.

Each oppression is also unique and needs to be understood in its uniqueness. RCers need to master the knowledge of these particular characteristics. Some examples would be the "settling for less" conditioning of women by sexist oppression or the denial of education and information to U.S. black people by white racism. It is desirable for an RCer to become an expert on the oppression of every group of which she or he is not a member (in order to be of decisive assistance against the internalized oppression of members of the group) and to become an expert on combatting the internalized oppression of her or his own group.

Some particular oppressions play key roles in the overall structure of the oppressive society and in relationship to the other oppressions.

The oppression of the working classes, which is, in its foundations and at its core, economic exploitation, is the fundamental oppression in this society. The taking of the value they produce from the working persons who produce it by the persons who "own" is what the whole society is "all about." **All other oppressions were developed as means of enforcing class oppression, as means of dividing the economically-oppressed against each other so as to secure their submission to and compliance with their economic exploitation.** This began in the first slave societies and continues to the present day. Working people are divided on lines of gender, on lines of age, on lines of race, physical ability, size, presence or absence of physical disability, sexual preference, religion, nationality, culture, and language, and are turned to oppressing each other and thus discouraged from uniting against the economic exploitation.

In this period, racism is the oppression that most widely interferes with human progress. Racism confuses and complicates efforts to overcome other oppressions: sexism, economic discrimination, religious intolerance, and so on. Because of this, the elimination of racism is the key struggle in this period. Ending racism will release enormous initiative for progress.

The oppression of young people by adults is the "training ground" for all other oppressions. If adults did not install powerlessness patterns early in the life of each young person, if the young person's submission was not enforced during this early time of physical smallness, insufficient information, dependence on others, and naive expectations of good treatment from surrounding humans, then later oppressions would be difficult or impossible to install. **The patterns laid in by the mistreatment of young people by adults are used as a foundation for the installation of all the other patterns of oppression.**

Oppression of Jews (anti-Semitism) in the Western and Arab countries plays the role of a "precedent-setter" or an "entering wedge," for the use of violence against all oppressed groups in times of social crisis. The oppression of Chinese in Southeast Asia and of East Indians in the countries of East Africa is very similar.

Classically, Jews have been a visible, distinct minority population in the countries of their exile with a highly developed culture and skills of survival. They, or their leaders, have been required to function as a tool of the ruling groups of the majority population as a condition of the Jews as a whole being tolerated. At the same time a continual low-level, "unofficial" campaign of anti-Jewish propaganda is carried out among the oppressed majority population. In times of threatened revolt by the oppressed people of the majority population, this unofficial campaign is replaced with violent official anti-Jewish propaganda. Pogroms, massacres, and expulsions are organized to turn the resentments of the oppressed majority population, which was on the point of rising against the oppressors, against the Jews (or Chinese or East Indians), using them as scapegoats. This tactic has been used over and over and over again in the last two thousand years. When the oppressors have diverted the revolutionary fervor of the oppressed into such shameful activity, it leaves the people who threatened rebellion ashamed of themselves and discouraged, and the Jews dispersed and plundered. Later the Jews are forced to be re-instated back into the role of visible agents of the oppressors, either in the country of the violence or in the place to which they've emigrated.

This scapegoating imposed upon Jews (and upon East Indians and Chinese in the other sections of the world) has been possible in the past in part because there was no homeland nation with power to support the Jewish populations in other countries, and the homeland nations of the Chinese and East Indians were under colonial domination and so almost powerless to protect their émigrés on the world scene.

Ending one oppression requires ending all oppressions. **Eliminating any one oppression—thoroughly, completely—requires eliminating all oppressions.** No one is free as long as there is one person oppressed. This appeals to our intuition, but it is also very practical. Any example of oppression going on with another group of people drags down and fetters our own struggle repeatedly. The white male working-class movement has continually floundered and weakened itself, in every practical sense, by going along with sexism, by going along with racism.

In the feudal society of the southern United States between the post-Civil War Reconstruction period and the Second World War, the enmities assiduously cultivated between the white sharecroppers and the black sharecroppers (the serfs of this feudal economy) kept both groups viciously and perpetually oppressed. Neither group could move out of the bondage as long as they tolerated the bondage of the others.

Any phenomenon can be understood better if it is examined from a variety of viewpoints. This has been recognized, at least partially, in a number of places besides RC. Start with the trivial example that it is better to walk around a house that is white on your side before you say confidently that "the house is white." Another side may very well be painted red. In the development of science, of mathematics, of literature and art, it happens over and over again that the knowledge about a certain subject is pronounced "complete." Then someone looks at the subject from an entirely new viewpoint and there is great excitement in the field as tremendous quantities of knowledge proceed to develop from the new viewpoint.

Looking back, we have looked at Re-evaluation Counseling from many different viewpoints as it has progressed and evolved. An early view, and still a beginning view for many people who come into Co-Counseling, is that RC is something that will make one feel better. This has certainly motivated many of us to have our first session or kept us going until we had our first good session. Later, when we tackle a chronic distress recording, we discover a new viewpoint and think of counseling as a way to help us think better and function better but not necessarily to feel better immediately.

We have moved through a number of viewpoints. The important viewpoint of the last couple of years is that **RC theory and practice is the uncovering and revealing of reality.** RC acts to strip the pseudo-reality from reality, rolls back the false reality which has occluded reality for us almost all our lives. The pseudo-reality has accumulated from the falsehoods, the invalidations, the pain, the unwarranted assumptions, which have been presented to us as reality, assumptions that we are helpless, that white people are smarter than people of color, that women's place is behind the kitchen stove, that working people are dumb, and so on. There are also much more subtle ones, such as the great foundation of liberal philosophy that "it is all hopeless but we must still do our best." From one viewpoint, Re-evaluation Counseling is the stripping off of the false reality which has been imposed by patterns, oppression, and mis-information and the revealing of the actual nature of the reality in which we function.

The attitude of powerlessness is almost universal. Even our RCers who have been raised to be "owning class" or to "rule" have a very limited concept of power. It may seem to those of us "raised poor" that owning-class people feel very powerful in their patterns compared to the way we feel in the patterns we wear, but theirs is a very limited concept of power. **The attitude of powerlessness conditioned on all humans is a fraud, imposed by distress and concealing an actuality of total power for any individual or rational group.**

Our power can be reclaimed. We are pointing at it as a goal, and we are coming closer in practice. Just the insight, just grasping the concept of total power immediately strengthened a whole number of other work fronts. Commitments began to work much better with the concept of the reality of reclaimable total power in the background. Our work against oppression got stronger. It is as if reaching for power "put lead in the pencil" of a lot of our previously discovered concepts. To actually reach for power itself leads to a much more effective scorning and discharging of fear. Reaching for power has not been well demonstrated, as yet. I have been trying to sound powerful before workshops and to get other people to at least sound powerful.

If any one individual reclaims her or his power and moves, that one individual can guarantee the future of the world. One such example will undoubtedly bring everyone else out of the timid bushes to fall in behind, ready to take charge of things.

It is always good if we can find a little gleam of light in the culture, a little crack in the pseudo-reality toward these concepts of reality that we are uncovering. The fact that even one individual acting out of confidence in her power will draw the necessary forces to her automatically is exemplified for me, at least a little bit, by a scene in a Charlie Chaplin movie (I think *Modern Times*). Unemployed Charlie, good-hearted, earnest, stands bewildered in a street filled with unemployed people. A truck comes by with a red cloth fastened to a stick protruding from the back, warning of a long load. The truck hits a bump and the stick with the red cloth falls off. Charlie notices it, rushes out onto the street, grabs the stick with the red cloth on it, and runs after the truck to return it, but they don't hear him and the truck goes off. The little tramp puts the stick over his shoulder and walks on disconsolately. The camera shows him walking on and on, but a sound begins and gets louder, and finally you recognize it as the tramp of feet, and the camera swings past Charlie, and thousands of people are marching behind him, following him and his flag.

These other concepts about reality lead to the big one. **Reality is benign.** In these efforts toward uncovering reality that we call RC we have drilled test wells through the grubby pseudo-reality in a number of places. RC began with one little piece of pseudo-reality being challenged. My first client was, fortunately, balanced just right between deep distress, classified as hopeless by professionals, and an eagerness to discharge, so that, in spite of my misguided efforts (misguided by the pseudo-reality that I, too, had accepted that if people are crying the most helpful thing you can do for them is to stop them), no matter how many times I stopped him and he agreed to stop, if I took any initiative he started crying again. From underneath the pseudo-reality, that said that to assist someone who is crying is to stop him or her from crying came the gleam of reality that if people are crying it is good for them to let them cry.

We drilled holes in the pseudo-reality in other areas. How can you motivate children to learn? There were some "enlightened" theories from wide-world attempts in this field that you praise them for "good" results. You criticize them not too unkindly when they don't shape their letters right, but you praise them if they get them facing the right way; you encourage them to do art as long as it is "reasonable" and "really means something," but you encourage them not to waste their time with "scrawls" you don't like. That got challenged. People thought a little beyond that. Praise everything they do. Don't pay much attention to it, just praise it with glassy eyes. That was a little better. Thinking crept on. Finally, we drilled all the way and the concept arose that if you just make the information available, children will themselves decide what they want to learn, how they want to learn it, and what is exciting for them. Everything fell into place—reality recognized at last, although not yet widely practiced.

Wherever we drilled a test hole in the pseudo-reality by challenging it, and wherever we dared punch the hole deep enough, sunshine, fresh air, bright colors, flowers, good sense drifted through. There was apparently something different on the other side. It was much better than the globby guck we were used to living with.

Any of the non-benign appearances of the pseudo-reality that hides reality, including the most threatening, the most horrifying, can be faced clearly, can be contradicted, can be discharged on, and can be eliminated. We do not have to wall off from our attention or thinking any of the negative concepts or the negative appearances of the pseudo-reality even though we have been trained or conditioned to avoid them.

I think this is quite important. Consider death. We have already done some work towards challenging this. The phenomenon of death can be faced clearly, and the fears of death can be discharged. Consider the Nazi holocaust—the genocidal holocaust of the Gay people, the gypsies, the Jews, the militant trade unionists. Too horrible to be thought about? No. In practice we have found that this horror can be contradicted, that discharge can be obtained, and that it can be thorough. Any particular clump of pseudo-reality, including the most threatening, such as terror of nuclear holocaust, can be faced, can be contradicted, can be discharged, and can be eliminated.

We do not need to avoid facing the most threatening clumps of the pseudo-reality by turning instead to ones we can face more easily, either as a priority or as a comfort or avoidance of the severe ones. We have the resources at this point. (We did not have them in the past or we would have come to this point earlier.) We have the resources, both in insights and in the advanced emergence of large numbers of people, so that we can now face the most threatening aspects of the patterns. If we do this, we can then relate to the more localized, not-quite-as-intimidating aspects and deal with those at the same time with even greater power.

The conclusion we reached was that we have to deal with everything. We must deal with where our next meal is coming from and we must prevent nuclear holocaust. We have a whole spectrum of issues that have to be dealt with. Even for the person who has starvation staring him or her in the face, the issue of eliminating nuclear weapons must be faced when there is slack to do so.

We have slack. We have an opportunity to think, an opportunity to work out policy that can mean a lot to all the people of the world, that can perhaps be crucial. We must not allow one concern to reject the others. We must not allow our concern for one situation and our need to do something about it to allow us to, in effect, reject thinking about nuclear holocaust and discharging our fears of that.

Now to the concepts relating to counseling itself. **Discharge and thinking can and should take place simultaneously.** If we fully grasp this, it can revolutionize the practical work of our counseling. Passive counseling (by which I mean only listening) may be a necessary stage in a counselor learning not to make patterned interventions into the counseling relationship, but this is only a learning stage.

The possibilities became clear with the exchange of commitments. Those of you who have seen two people exchange their commitments well have noticed that as the roles of client and counselor shift back and forth, the counseling gets sharper and sharper. Generally, the person who is counselor is shaking, too, while the one in the client role cries, shakes, and laughs with an occasional yawn. As soon as the roles switch, however, the new counselor keeps shaking (and crying a little bit perhaps) but pays very keen attention. As the roles shift back and forth, the relationship obviously works better and better the more they do it, because they are thinking better and are getting more attention from each other. This seems to be because we have developed a situation where thinking and discharge can take place simultaneously, and *this allows us to realize that they always should.*

Actively thinking, and intervening, within the correct role of the counselor, is necessary for the counselor or the counseling to be fully effective. We correctly say that when you are in trouble, when you don't know what to do, go back to just listening and most of the time if you really listen, the client will find a way to get to the discharge. All this has been correct. But it is not the fundamental role of the counselor to be passive.

The actual relationship between the client and the counselor includes two fully active, fully thinking, fully participating people.

We will continue to lay emphasis in the early stages of learning to counsel on the counselor "shutting up" and listening and paying attention, because almost all of us come to learn counseling with very bad habits of "shooting our faces off," offering opinions, intervening thoughtlessly, taking the client's role away from our client by "remembering" an experience like the one she or he is telling about and interrupting the client's narrative with our own. (All of these can be viewed as unaware and disruptive attempts to force some clienting for oneself.) When we start out to be a counselor, we're so conditioned and so desperate that we continually interrupt, intervene, make comments, and pass judgments, and do other unworkable things. So, in the early stages of learning to counsel, it has been correct to be fiercely insistent that the counselor only listen, and be interested, and pay as much attention as she or he can, at that point.

In later practice, however, we must move more and more toward an active role for a counselor as we become more experienced and better counselors. I give support from the expression on my face, from the tone of my voice, by the way I'm holding the person, by my cheek against his or hers, by the bit of poetry I remember to quote that will contradict the distress. I do a great array of things, actively. We need to say clearly that the passive role of the counselor is a learning stage—a powerful, effective one to be reverted to in many situations, especially when we have not yet paid enough attention to the client to know accurately what the distress is.

These are the full roles of Co-Counseling: a very active, thinking-all-the-time-as-well-as-discharging client, a very active, thinking-all-the-time and actively-intervening-against-the-distress, skillful counselor.

The word from outside the pattern, or outside the oppression, can have great, almost unlimited effectiveness in contradicting distress.

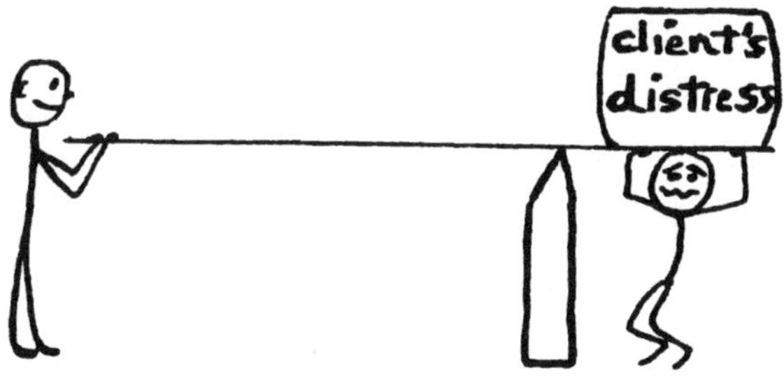

I've used the sketch at workshops of a long lever arm, with a weight representing a load of distress sitting on one end of the lever. The client stands underneath the weight, pushing up against it with no leverage. The fulcrum or balance point of the lever is very near to that weight.

The carefree, untrammeled counselor stands at the other end of the lever, with great leverage for dealing with and contradicting the weight of the client's distress.

The client is always a perfect client. We have advanced this statement in recent times, and I think it's been helpful. It has interrupted the sneaky practice of blaming the client for poor counseling. As counselors, we had best assume that if the client could do any better, he or she would be doing it, but that our intervention from the freedom of the counselor's role always has many more possibilities and opportunities than we have used at any time.

Any intelligence always has freedom to operate from a different viewpoint than any previously adopted, or than is suggested by others, or than is attempted to be enforced on the person by any force outside the person's intelligence. Viewpoint always remains the free choice of the individual. This always-present freedom to choose one's viewpoint places the reclaiming of power within reach of any individual in any situation.

We always have freedom to choose our viewpoint. This freedom cannot be denied to us, no matter how much the pseudo-reality tries to insist that it can. Thought control never worked, even with huge secret police forces. It never worked. "Die Gedanken sind frei." Thinking is free. You may tie me up, blindfold me and gag me, encompass me with irons and sink me in the depths of the deepest sea, but as long as I'm thinking, you cannot tell me what to think. In particular, you cannot take away my freedom to choose my own viewpoint.

A quick inspiration from the first faculty workshop has become a small classic. It's been repeated many times. Suppose you're on a jet plane. You're sitting near the emergency exit. It fails. The pressure in the cabin blows you out at 41,000 feet. Will you despair? You may, if you wish, but what good will that do? You still have freedom to choose a different viewpoint. You can unzip your jacket, spread it for a pair of wings, look for the nearest body of water, steer toward it, enjoy the unusual view you have of the world during the next five minutes, and calculate the best angle of approach to the surface of that water. It may not work, but what have you lost? If you choose despair, what have you gained? At the very least you'll have a much more interesting five minutes.

Beyond its philosophical support, this is a powerful counseling tool. Insistence on a change of viewpoint for the client by the counselor can heave the great bulk of distress up out of the mud.

Any client's fear can be scorned effectively by the counselor, and this will lead to its discharge by the client. "Scorning fear" has become a slogan. By this we mean not respecting fear, treating fear with contempt, with amused derision. Workable practice consists of the counselor taking an unafraid attitude toward the client's fear.

As in most counseling, tone of voice, facial expression, and the communication of relaxed confidence is very important.

To get started, we're going to have to be a little daring. When the client says, "I'm afraid of death," we can say in a relaxed way, "That's interesting. Do you think you'll ever die?" and if the client says mumble, mumble, we can happily say, "Well, you probably will," and the tension will get contradicted and the client will begin discharging. In order to get restimulated by our client's fear, we have to identify our fear with the client's fear. This takes a lot of work. We have to make a great effort to restimulate our fear by our client's fear. We think it's automatic, but that isn't so. It takes a lot of effort.

To use "opposite" words to contradict a pattern seems an obvious thing to do, but it works in general only with the most eager or with the most shut-down clients. The reason why it doesn't work most of the time is that the client has been trying to do this for years, and the whole area has become calloused. "I am no good," "I am good," "I am no good," goes the internal argument with the pattern. This has been going on for years, and the entire area is numb. All the pattern's defenses are over here resisting this approach. If you ask the person to say, "I am good," the pattern's voice will say, "Aw, to heck with that; I'm no good and I know it." However, if you ask, "Would you say, 'Once upon a time I had a small, good intention, even though I couldn't carry it out'?" the pattern isn't set for that, the slight contradiction slips in, and the client begins to discharge.

E— was set to lead a group of women feeling that they weren't good looking anymore when they got older, and she did a great job of exhorting them to resist those feelings: "What has been your big experience against it? I think we should just take a stand against this!" There wasn't a lot of discharge, so I butted in. I asked her to admit that she was ugly. I didn't look at her like I thought she was ugly, and I had enough of a relationship with her that she knows I don't think she's ugly. However, the idea of lightheartedly counting the wrinkles and the crow's feet became very, very funny, and she got more and more beautiful by the minute. The only thing that was threatening her with ugliness was the strain on her face from defensively insisting that she wasn't ugly. She looks just wonderful this morning.

If we get rigid as we try to contradict the client's pattern, and we think, "Ah ha, here it is, a brick wall in plain sight. How does one contradict that brick wall? Ah ha, client, lower your head and butt that wall," we wind up blaming the client because the client looks at the contradiction we suggest and says, "Uh uh. No thank you." If we insist that the client does it, he or she does it numbly, unawarely. He or she is mainly occupied with thoughts about how stupidly we're counseling him or her. We forget that a pattern cannot bear any contradiction. If the pattern says, "I'm no good," and you can, instead, offer the suggestion that you had a vague report that they were one millionth of one percent not bad, the pattern will begin to discharge. Once you get discharge started, you can add more contradiction, and keep piling it on, but keep them believable contradictions.

This is what's wrong with the heavy-handed contradiction. It isn't believable. A client says, "I'm no good," and you say, "I want you to say, 'I'm the most wonderful person that ever lived,'" and he or she looks at you like you're out of your mind. It's impossible for the client to get any belief through the heaviness.

Question: It's not clear how what you said contradicted "ugly."

HJ: The pattern was not, by this time, "feeling ugly." It was "defending against the possibility of being ugly"—a defensive posture. That was the pattern. If, when you look at it, you conclude that the pattern was one of "feeling ugly," you miss the boat. All her dramatizations were a defense against considering the possibility of ugliness, see? So I got her to quit defending. I asked, "How's your ugliness this morning?"—and discharge started. Now, a week or two later, I may drop by and say, "I've always thought you were beautiful," just to remove any lingering invalidation that might have stuck in there. But the point is that you contradict the actual distress.

E—: You did say afterwards that I was good-looking.

HJ: A little bit. *(E— laughs; group laughter.)* Now she laughed much harder at that than if I had passionately insisted that she was beautiful, because my tone of voice indicates that I do not share her tension about her looks. That's the big thing. When I tell J— I don't care if she dies or not, there may be a little wince ("My God, Harvey, I thought you were my buddy"), but the main thing is, somebody in the situation doesn't share her worries about dying. That's why she laughed a little bit, and if we'd kept on with it, there'd be shakes.

"A commitment" is a serious promise to act at all times against a particular distress. Such a commitment accelerates re-emergence. That's a short description, but it touches the heart of the meaning of the very powerful commitment. It is a promise to take the direction of one's life away from the pattern, a promise made to be kept, not just used in session, but to be kept all the time.

To exchange commitments between two counselors in a session or series of sessions is to simultaneously enhance thinking and discharging by both parties and continually increase the safety in the relationship. I'm talking now about the exchanged commitment. It's extremely powerful. How can one refrain from doing it all the time? I don't know, but I forget to do it!

The goal of immortality, taken seriously, contradicts and permits the discharge of important distress for every client. It will certainly enhance the possibility of, and may possibly lead to, immortality, to living indefinitely. (See the journal *Forever and Ever* No. 1 for more details.)

The explosively restimulating character of sexual distress in our present cultures may be safely defused (that is, the restimulating propensity may be contained), and the distress discharged, through persistent counseling restricted to the earliest sexual memories, the earliest memories connected to sex in any way at all. This is the safe path through one of the stickiest swamps that we have to traverse.

Relationship expectations between humans need to be carefully defined by each person in the relationship, with each one's separate expectations clearly stated by each party, and the subset of those that can be agreed upon clearly defined in order for the relationship to operate well. Each of us brings his or her own definition of what he or she expects from the relationship to the other person, and assumes, without the slightest shred of evidence, that this is what the other person expects and agrees to. Often the two sets of expectations have very little in common. Carefully spelling out each set and finding out which expectations are in common, and agreeing upon those and agreeing not to agree on the others, not to try to fulfill the others, is crucial to a good relationship.

Rational close friendships with many members of the other gender are desirable and possible of attainment for any woman or any man. (Beginning theory on this is in *The Reclaiming of Power*, p. 161, "Close Friendships Between Women and Men." I refer you to that article for expansion of this point.)

A clear statement, written in the first place by the counselor, of the reality of the client's life history, goals, and relationship to the total environment, written from a position of triumphant appreciation and eager expectation (a framework), will enhance and stabilize the re-emergence of the client.

The "panel" presentation greatly enhances communication across oppression barriers. This is an arrangement for representatives of oppressed groups to speak directly to the general population and to each other on six points: (1) What's been positive about being Wygelian, a member of the group from which you speak? (I say "Wygelian" to mean a member of any oppressed group.) Inside the oppression which you have endured, what's been positive about being a Wygelian? (2) What's been hard about being a Wygelian? (3) Why are you proud of being a Wygelian? (4) What do Wygelians wish other people understood about them? (5) What do Wygelians want other people never to say or do again? (6) What do Wygelians require of others if they're to be effective allies for Wygelians?

Any person's functioning in any job will improve if the person can be listened to with attention by fellow workers while she or he speaks to (a) her or his strong points in the job and (b) needed

improvements, and then hears the others' comments on the same two points. Self-estimation is a very powerful process. We have shown this to be true with RC leaders for years and have it in our Guidelines. It is also a tool that people will eagerly use in work situations in the wide world. To use your counseling skills during a lunch hour chat, to bring out how each one is a good worker, and how each one does a good job and how it could be improved, is to unleash great forces for unity, communication, and self-esteem among workers.

To blame another human for one's distresses or troubles is to accept powerlessness for oneself. Essentially, I have noticed that, among thousands of clients, the ones who blame and reproach others for their distress, even if their blames and reproaches are restricted to the actual agents of the hurts that were put on them or the ones who actually perpetrated the hurts on them, are in trouble. They sometimes seem to have an easier life, they seem to be comfortable blaming others, they seem to be carefree compared to the rest of us. Yet they pay a very, very heavy price for it in powerlessness.

Those, on the other hand, who decided not to put reproaches or blame on anyone else, not to pass on the hurt, but to accept the responsibility for dealing with it, even though they sometimes mistakenly blame themselves a lot in the process and sometimes seem to have tougher lives, live longer and everybody likes them better. They're much closer to re-emergence. I don't know what to suggest that you do with this, except perhaps to recommend that you and your Co-Counselors examine any points in your life where you decided your difficulties were someone else's fault and direct special attention to discharging those, so that you get your full integrity back a little faster.

A good theory arouses much greater expectations than its practice currently satisfies, and this is desirable for the growth of both the theory and the practice. The gap between the expectations which our theory arouses, and the achievements which our practice furnishes, has been the excuse for a great deal of expressed disappointment, inactivity, and even hostility from some former or present Co-Counselors. Perhaps this disappointment can be avoided by clear communication in the beginning that this gap exists and that as our practice improves, our theory is also going to improve and stay ahead of the practice. Trying to close that gap is what improves the practice of counseling, but this is the responsibility of the person, himself or herself, and it is not the responsibility of the Community or other Co-Counselors to do it for him or her without the person's own efforts. Such disappointment is not realistic.

There are no "shoulds" in the universe—no obligations. You do not "owe" anyone anything. Your own fresh thinking will always lead you to do a better job for yourself and others than any "shoulds" which you try to live up to. This is very close to your freedom to choose your own viewpoint. People seem able to hear and act upon the insight that "There are no shoulds in the universe."

Trust your own thinking. No one else's thinking about you and your affairs can possibly be accurate enough and well-informed enough about you to be a guide for your decisions. (The only situations in which you should ever follow someone else's thinking about you is in accepting a direction to contradict a chronic pattern; and even here the direction should bring discharge in a reasonable amount of time to continue to be accepted.)

Trust your own thinking. It will take thoughtful examination of your thinking to distinguish between your thinking and your patterned compulsions or assumptions, but you will always be able to tell the difference if you check.

Trust your own thinking. You will make mistakes if you do anything meaningful at all, but if you are acting on your own thinking, the results will quickly be noticed by you and you will correct the mistake promptly. If you have accepted someone else's thinking as your guide, you have already stopped thinking for yourself, and the mistakes will go uncorrected much longer.

Trust your own thinking. Trust your intuitions. Check on, but respect, your hunches, your "gut feelings."

Trust your own thinking.

The Art of Listening

A talk to the Merced County (California, USA)
Mental Health Association
November 7, 1981
—Harvey Jackins

I and a group of my friends have, for about thirty-one years, been trying to develop and expand and improve a system for people relating to each other helpfully. For the last eleven years our efforts have gone beyond the city of Seattle and in that time have spread to nearly every state in the Union, nearly every large city in the United States, most Canadian provinces, and about thirty-eight other countries. We've had an explosive expansion. Our understanding of the subject continually improves. There are new developments all the time. It's challenging to stay on top of what we are learning.

There are many ways of approaching what we have named "Re-evaluation Counseling." One way is to ask you to look at what happens whenever people are together and have a chance to talk, at times when they're not completely preoccupied with their jobs or other activity. If you will think back to the coffee-shop, picnic table, or similar situations, you will remember that people are, everywhere and at all times when in the presence of each other, either trying to be listened to—talking every chance they get—or waiting patiently or impatiently for a chance to interrupt any other person who is talking and start talking themselves.

Think about this. You will find that whenever people are together, they're making an effort to be listened to, and *are* very seldom listened to, because the person that they are trying to get to listen to them is waiting desperately and impatiently for a chance to be listened to himself or herself.

SOMEONE MUST LISTEN

If we were to encapsulate what we have learned to do in a sentence or two—and there's much more, there are many complicated applications that come from it—it is to explain to people that what they are trying to do all the time, this trying to be listened to, is a very profound process. It will have profound results if it ever gets a chance to operate and it will operate, *if they will take turns.* They need to just take turns, and agree, "Yes, I *will* listen to you and really pay attention to you for a while, if you will give me a chance to do the same thing later on." We call that "Co-Counseling." The awkward word "counseling" meant "giving advice" to most people when we first started using it, but it has now come to have a good deal of the meaning we've used for it in the intervening thirty-one years, which does not mean "giving advice" at all, but basically *listening and paying attention.*

This inherent process that we're all equipped to use has been, in general, frustrated, simply because it takes another person outside of ourselves really paying attention while we talk and think about ourselves, and re-experience the distresses that we have accumulated, for it to work.

OUR ESSENTIAL NATURE IS FINE

The reality seems to be that human beings are essentially quite wonderful, and they climb their way back to practicing that wonderfulness whenever they get a chance. It's true that we've inherited a physiological set-up from our pre-human ancestors that has a lot of instincts and physical determinants in it, but we've also developed a mind, an ability to think, that is almost unique in the kingdom of life on this planet. (Some of us assume, of course, that we have older brothers and sisters somewhere out there in the Galaxy who will arrive in a space ship any day now and give us a hand, but they haven't gotten here yet.) This ability to think is quite remarkable.

We define "intelligence" as the ability to come up with a brand-new, accurate response for each new situation, to never use an old response for a new situation, because a new situation is new, and if you try to use something that worked fine for a previous situation, it's not going to quite fit the new situation, which never occurred before. There aren't any identical entities in the universe, not even two electrons are absolutely identical, and so two environmental situations for a human being will never be exact replicas of each other. There will always be something new. When we're functioning on this particular human ability, this flexible intelligence of ours, we're quite capable of taking in all the information of a situation, comparing it with the information from past experiences that we've understood, noting the similarities, noting the differences, putting together a response that is similar to what handled similar experiences in the past, but is modified to allow for the differences in this situation, and, being exactly accurate, handling each new situation well.

This ability seems to spring out of the colossal central nervous system we have. No one yet really knows how it works, but we're creeping up on it. Scientists who have spent their lives examining the central nervous system are beginning to get some vague idea. It's worthwhile noting that of the forty billion neurons (forty billion or so—I don't think anybody's counted them exactly) that each of us possesses, only a few hundred are occupied in bringing information in to the central nervous system from the sense organs, from the excellent battery of sense organs we have. Only a few hundred of these neurons bring information in, and a few hundred more transmit orders out from the central nervous system to the glands and the muscles. The rest of the forty billion sit there and talk to each other. There's a tremendous interconnection. We're very complex. We're all justified in feeling quite good about ourselves, because the goofiest mistake we ever made was really an enormous triumph of complex behavior. There's nothing simple about us.

OUR INTELLIGENCE CAN BE INTERRUPTED

This ability to come up with fresh, new answers, this rational human intelligence of ours, gets interrupted by situations of stress, of painful emotion, or of pain. Any kind of physical hurt or emotional hurt interrupts this, to a greater or lesser degree. Under those situations, the information coming in from the environment, which ordinarily is handled very easily and in great volume by our tremendous intelligence, doesn't get sorted out, doesn't get understood, doesn't get compared and contrasted with what we already know, nor filed away to be useful information. Instead it congeals, and this unevaluated information becomes, in effect, a recording of what went on during the bad times, and this recording persists. It includes the ineffective behavior, the distressed feelings, *and* the shutting down of our thinking.

We have the abilities to take such a distress recording apart (that's the principal message I have, how to take it apart, or how to encourage its being taken apart, since the process is quite spontaneous and inherent), but since this recovery ability, the recovery mechanism, the healing process is usually interfered with by social conditioning, the congealed, not-understood information from a distressed experience instead remains a recording of bad feelings and a compulsive pattern of behavior. When reminded of it enough (the folk saying goes, "It reminds me too much of,") by similarities in a new situation, we are thrown into a repetition of the inability to think that the original hurt caused, and so we act rigidly, unsuccessfully, uncomfortably, and, usually, unawarely in the new situation. This allows additional distresses to accumulate and mount up.

PEOPLE ARE GOOD

This notion of the distress recording, the congealed results of an experience of distress that was not allowed to be taken apart and re-evaluated, is a very simple but very profound explanation of all the things that have puzzled us about people. Each one of us knows—and I remind you of this—that he or she is really a good person. You have been told you're not, and in the presence of fresh criticism you get to feeling you're not, but in your heart of hearts you know you're a good person, that you've always done the very best you could, *and that is true.* Each of us knows that he or she is much smarter than he or she can often show, that he or she has a lot of intelligence that doesn't come out in the tension of the final exam, or the upsetting situation, *and this is true.* I now tell you that what you know about yourself is also true of everyone else. This profound knowledge that you've hidden to escape ridicule—that you're a good person, that you always do your best, and that you're much smarter than you sometimes act or than people think—*this is true, not only of you, but of other people as well.*

THE RECOVERY PROCESSES

This wonderful nature of ours that gets obscured in this way would resurge, can resurge, and will resurge, if particular processes are allowed to take place. These are what we call "discharge." "Discharge" is a general word to encompass some very profound processes that are dependably characterized outwardly by tears, by crying, by trembling, by laughing (in many forms), by angry storming, by yawns, by non-repetitive, eager talk. These processes melt the rigidities of the distress pattern and turn its contents back into the useful information it should have been in the first place. These processes also free this tremendous intellect of ours, this flexible behavior of ours, to operate. Any discharge—any tears, any trembling, any laughter, any storming, any yawns (yawning is the dependable indication of the release of physical distress)—tends to move us back to functioning on our original nature, which is that of a genius-sized intelligence and a very good person and (more and more we're realizing this) a very *powerful* person. The powerlessness with which most of us feel infected ("I can't," "I wish I could," "I have to wait," and "Somebody will tell me I can someday") is all acquired. We're all conceived, and most of us are born, with a sense of being able to do anything. This is closer to the actual reality, and only the social conditioning has obscured this—the tremendous amounts of oppression that are ladled upon us systematically.

ACCIDENTS AND CONTAGION

The distress patterns that we acquire, the inhibiting fences that get built around us, come partly from accidental hurts. There are such things as slipping and falling and hurting oneself. In greater volume they come from the contagion of this distress. The person who was hurt is pulled by the resulting distress pattern, in some situations, to hurt someone else. The little boy who was beaten by his father is pulled, when he becomes a father himself, to beat his son in the same way and pass the hurt on. There's a certain contagion in the distress.

SYSTEMATIC OPPRESSION ALSO

More and more as we explore the phenomenon, and find our way out from under these intimidating loads of distress, we realize that there's also a *systematic* process of imposing hurts operating in this society. An oppressive society systematically places hurts upon people in order to condition them to fill certain rigid, submissive roles, or, in some cases, certain dominating, oppressive roles. We've learned in the last few years, and can now state with great confidence, that no one would submit to being oppressed if distress patterns were not first installed. We would not permit being placed in any of the victim roles of oppression. (We're all oppressed—we're oppressed as workers, we're oppressed as women, we're oppressed as children, we're oppressed by racism, we're oppressed by many other oppressions.) None of us would accept any of these oppressions except that we were first hurt as children so early that we were unable to resist, and the groundwork of distress patterns was laid in for imposing additional new oppressions as we grew older. More than that, and this is very hopeful, *no one would play an oppressor role* otherwise. No man would act in a sexist way to women, unless he had first been hurt and then manipulated into the other end of the oppression. No aristocrat would ever condescendingly mistreat the common folk if not first mistreated while young. (In England this shows up very strikingly. The young aristocrats are sent to special schools and deliberately hurt there to prepare them for their roles when older. It's always easier to see in somebody else's society than it is in our own.)

MANY ARE LEARNING

This great weight of distress patterns that has limited us and has frustrated us and that hangs over us like a pall—every once in a while getting us down real hard, and then lifting somewhat as we climb out again and function, always limiting us, always making us feel that we must accept some limited role in society because we're female, or because we're young, or because our folks worked with their hands, or whatever the oppression is—this can be and is being thrown off by an increasing number of people at this point. Since Re-evaluation Counseling spread beyond Seattle, we have reached in some fashion—through fundamentals classes or lectures or support groups—about a half-million people. It's been a very rapid development.

We've transcended many barriers. We had no written literature to start with. Now there are twelve or thirteen books. We publish twenty-five magazines irregularly. There is a special magazine for women, a special magazine for working-class people, for blacks, for Latino/as, a magazine for people of Asian inheritance, a young people's magazine, one for "mental health" workers. It's called *Recovery and Re-emergence,* and it exchanges information among Re-evaluation Counselors who are working in the "mental health" field.

We've learned a lot; but all we've learned rests on this fairly simple re-discovery, and all the progress is based on this foundation: if at least two people will take turns, and one or more of them will listen, remarkable and good changes will take place with the person who is being listened to.

CONTENT IS UNIVERSAL

Every time we take Re-evaluation Counseling into a new country or cross another language barrier or begin to work in a new culture, we are likely to be told that this "doesn't fit into our culture." It's true that some of the trappings that we bring in from the United States culture don't fit—we're often unaware of them until the new people point them out and help us peel them off—but also it's true that the fundamentals are universal. I was told very seriously that we could not reach Arab people by talking about the need for men to cry, because Arab men don't cry. (There's a certain point to that warning, because talking about Re-evaluation Counseling is often not the way to communicate it—you want to demonstrate it instead.) I have given about twelve Arab men their first counseling session, and ten of them cried very hard the first time.

The content of this healing relationship is universal. All humans are human. The cultural differences are interesting and rich, but any *divisions* between us on the basis of culture are completely unjustified. All of us are very, very human. I remember working as a counselor in the developing years of Re-evaluation Counseling. Many of my clients were women, and as they opened up and told me all about themselves, I realized with growing surprise that women are just like men. I had never suspected that before! We're engaged currently in trying to break down the barriers that have developed between men and women, and are working to achieve closer friendships between women and men. Women are listening with amazement as they discover that men are just like women!

If you can just listen, that's good. Beginning Co-Counselors often cannot listen well, because of the internal pressure to talk themselves. When it's their turn to listen, they say, okay, go ahead, but are still very inattentive (demonstrates bad attention). Often the persons they are "listening" to are so desperate to be listened to that they pretend the other person is listening, and they have a great session! Later when better listening is needed, the second person has had a session and is not quite so inattentive, and the process improves. Co-Counseling is a sort of a mutual "take-turns" bootstrapping process. You can't lift yourself by your own boot straps but you can take turns lifting each other. It works, and of course it works in larger groups than two, but for the economy of time most Co-Counseling is done in pairs, switching roles between the first person who is listened to and the second, who listens. That's about what it amounts to.

PEOPLE ARE PEOPLE

We've tackled some very tough and complicated problems along the way. One was that we had to verify the generality of the recovery process. For a period in the early years of Re-evaluation Counseling I accepted very distressed people as clients. I had to guess as to how to handle them and made many mistakes, but I learned a great deal. Basically what I was trying to find out was, is there one kind of people who get put in mental institutions and another kind of people who can handle their lives? I had to find that out in practice. Theory wasn't enough. I'm very pleased to know, as I'm sure all of you already intuitively know, that there's only one kind of people. The person who seems to be in another strange category is someone who has been hurt very deeply, someone on whom a large load of distress has piled up, who has been, and often continues to be, oppressed very seriously. Given enough help (the word *enough* is important), anyone is able to climb all the way out to elegant functioning. Making that statement is fine, and I make it very positively. Doing it, of course, is another question, because it takes a lot of resource to support someone making a long climb back. This is no news to you who work in the "mental health" field.

HOW TO COUNSEL

We can say much more clearly now than we used to what it takes to be an effective listener for someone whom you wish to help (one-way), or with whom you wish to exchange help (two-way, as in Co-Counseling). It's very simple to say, and I'm pleased that I can say it this clearly after thirty-one years of saying it in many other ways. If you wish to help someone that you're going to listen to, plain listening is fine, but there are distresses that take a little more than that, and the more you can do beyond that, the more effective you will be.

You (a) pay enough attention to them, that you notice accurately what the distresses are. One of the ways of finding that out is to ask, "What's bothering you?", and then listen and they'll tell you. They'll never fail you. "What about yourself would you like to change?" "(Sigh) Well, no one ever asked me that before, but _____," and they will tell you.

If there is an inhibiting pattern in the way of them speaking out clearly to you, you can simply look at them, and the expression on their faces, the one that they wear when they're not crying or laughing or discharging in some other way, will tell you about their distress. It's a perfectly familiar expression, but it's not theirs. It's the expression of a chronic pattern that has grown there from the distress that has become chronic. It may be like this (demonstrates) or it may be like this (demonstrates) or whatever, but, whatever it's like, it will tell you something.

Look at the posture. Apparently the natural posture for a man is very close to this (demonstrates). How many men do you know who stand or sit like that? Most of them have been beaten down to a submissiveness posture. A few of them are stuck in defensive postures (demonstrates). How does a woman stand? Something like this (demonstrates). Yet, how many women stand so proudly? If you see one like that in a crowd once in a while, your eyes are drawn to her almost immediately. Almost all of us in our postures tell the chronic distresses that we bear and try to resist all the time. There are other clues in a person's appearance as well.

So, (a) you pay enough attention to the person to see what the distresses are. (b) You think, "How could those be contradicted?" That's demanding. You must actually think about him or her. Think, think. How can these distresses be contradicted?

(c) You contradict them. Just that. You contradict them. The person will discharge. He or she will talk eagerly, decidedly, alively. (Not "blah, blah, blah"—that kind of talk is just the rehearsal of a pattern with words in it.) They will talk eagerly, alively, or they will begin to laugh, they will begin to cry, they will begin to shake, they will begin to yawn—something will begin to happen if you do that. If these things don't happen you haven't contradicted the distress enough, that's all.

For many situations, simply to be listened to with interest and attention is enough contradiction. When was the last time anyone did that for you? Often discharge begins to occur simply with that. Beginning Co-Counselors sometimes have marvelous results with each other just by managing to keep their mouths shut for a little while. There's more to learn also, of course, and we're learning more all the time.

ATTITUDES TO ADOPT

There are certain additional, general things to learn, if you're going to be a good listener/friend (and I assume you are at least considering the possibility). There are certain general hurts that people have suffered from that can also be contradicted generally. There's a certain battery of attitudes that, if you can adopt them, will make you a more effective listener and friend than if you just sit there and clench your teeth to keep silent. These may be hard to adopt at first, but if you even try to act as if you held these attitudes, it will help. It will bring you out of some of your own ruts, and it will make you much more attractive and appealing as a listener to the person that you are listening to.

What are some of the attitudes that we can extend toward the person that we are listening to that will generally contradict their distresses? One of them is *approval*. I now look approvingly at you. Which of us ever felt very hurt while someone was approving of us? It may happen, but it's not common. Another is *delight*. I shall be delighted with you. Who was ever hurt at a time when someone was delighted with them? (Voice from audience: "Not me!") I won't say that I won't find an instance someday, but I haven't found one yet. Take an attitude of *respect*. Listen as if the person's words and what they have to say and how they are feeling are worthy of full consideration. Almost all distress carries with it disrespect. Certainly all the oppressions, which probably put a majority of our distress upon us, carry disrespect at their core.

In working with teenagers, the internalized oppression which takes places with every group that has been oppressed was so heavy that we were looking for a way of interrupting it. (This first occurred with a group in England, but it's worked with every group of young people we've tried it with since.) We asked them to make a promise to each other, and the wording is, "I solemnly promise that, from this moment on, I will never again treat any young person, including myself, with anything less than complete respect." We've never had a group of young people together where more than two of them have made that promise before everyone in the group started crying, got their arms around each other and sobbed. Lack of respect is a crucial element in the mistreatment which young people endure.

It's also at the heart of every other oppression. What's at the heart of sexism? A woman being treated without respect. What's at the heart of racism? The non-white being treated without respect. What's at the heart of ageism? The elder being treated as a cast-off. "Oh, Grandma, now you just go sit down." Lack of respect.

So, if, as a listener, you can adopt an attitude of full respect, let the person you are listening to feel that whatever he or she has to say is important, you will be more effective. What you hear should be listened to with respect, because either it will be thinking, and everyone's thinking is worthy of respect, or it will be some distress that the person is trying to voice in order to get it out there where she or he can see it and begin to take it apart, and that's very deserving of respect, also. If you can adopt an attitude of respect and keep adopting it until it becomes second nature, becomes a good habit, then your listening becomes more powerful.

CONFIDENCE FOR THEM

What else? What other hurts are so general that we can set up a general attitude to contradict them? How about confidence? How about being confident that the person you're listening to can attain what he or she wants? The person says, "I wish I could ______," and you say, "I think you can do it. I think you're just the person who can do it." If you maintain this attitude, can't you imagine the lift that will give? Very few people have had much confidence expressed in them. Even our beloved parents, who wanted so desperately to give us the best start in life they possibly could, had been so hurt themselves that often when they went to express confidence and support to us they instead gave us warnings. "Don't go too far," and "Don't stick your neck out," and "Try to get a good, steady job and hold on to it," and statements like that. We got their fears instead of their confidence. So, if you can express confidence, if you say to the person, "I know you can do it, I'm sure you'll succeed," it's going to help almost every time.

HIGH EXPECTATIONS

What other attitudes can we helpfully adopt? I think high expectations is one. Over and over I hear from clients, "I wasn't expected to do anything. I wanted to become a nuclear physicist, but everyone told me it would be a waste of time because I'd just get married and have a family anyway." So I offer the expectation—"Now your family is grown, you can go back to school and be a nuclear physicist if you want to. Don't you dare settle for anything less than what you want." I express that kind of attitude.

COMMITMENTS

On the drive up from Fresno, I helped someone practice a commitment. The commitment is a very powerful tool. It has to be just the right commitment. It has to be the person's own commitment. This commitment was: "I solemnly promise that from this moment on I will never again settle for anything less than everything." Sounds a little ambitious, doesn't it? But try it a few times. You'll be amazed at the thoughts that come winging through your head. In your role as the listener, in your role as the good friend, remember to have high expectations.

(Not reproaches! They're already too plentiful. "Why didn't you get a higher grade? Only an A+? Why didn't you get better than that?") Offer instead the confident expectation, "If you want it, you can get it, and I'll back you all the way." "You're not sure you can think well enough? I know you can think. Can you do what you want to? Yes, you can. There's no question about it."

If you remember that your goal is to be a good listener/friend and remember what a powerful force listening is, and if you then think of the attitudes you always wished somebody had taken toward you, you'll know what to do. You'll know the attitudes that your friend is waiting for. Confidence, respect, delight, safety, approval, awareness, reassurance that the person has always done his or her best, natural physical contact. Commitment. "I'll be with you. I'll stick with you, I won't abandon you no matter how hard the going gets." That may feel like an awful load, as if you listen to five people and you commit yourself, then you may have to be washing everybody's dishes next week—but it's not the same thing. If a pattern comes in to demand that you wash the dishes to prove you're really with them, you say, "I'm sorry, that's not what I really meant. I'm for *you*, not for your dirty dishes." The danger isn't as great as you may feel it is.

LOVE

There's a big attitude which we're all going to be awkward and scared about at first: love. Love. If you can look at the person you're listening to with full, warm, unabashed love, then all kinds of things become possible. Something happens (and I suspect some of you at least already know about this) when you listen really well to someone. As he or she opens up and is crying just as hard as he or she can, the real person shows. It's as if a screen rolls back with the tears or the laughter or trembling, and you really see the person, and you find yourself falling in love. That's good. Don't be scared. Be careful, but don't be scared. Don't be afraid to fall in love with each other. We have rules in the Co-Counseling Community that if you meet people as a Co-Counselor you do not go into business with them, you do not try to sell them life insurance, you do not romance them, or go off and marry them. But love them, yes. Love them thoroughly. The attitude of love improves your listening. Most of us are suffering from an inadequate chance to express love. Most of us are pent up with love that we don't have enough opportunity to express. It will be good for you.

The need to love is a much bigger rational need even than the need to be loved. Our culture emphasizes people needing to be loved, and that's real, but it's a small thing compared with the need *to love*. If you don't really let your love out, you're going to turn sour inside. So add the attitude of love to your listening. Work at it carefully, cautiously. Don't confuse it with doing each other's dishes. Just keep it what it is, just love, and it will improve. Some of you are "mental health" professionals, I'm sure, and you've been trained to sit on the other side of a desk and not get "involved" and I don't want to invalidate your training, but if you can have this overall attitude of love, it doesn't matter. You can stay on your stepladder if you have to and still love them, and every one of your clients or patients or whatever you call them, is going to know the difference right away. They're going to be emboldened to pick up their feet and walk right out of the swamp with great speed compared to what they would do otherwise.

Generally, I don't talk to people about one-way listening. That's a special problem. Generally I talk to people about *exchanging* this relationship, and that's the way I want to talk to you, too. Because, even if you have big case loads that you're working on, you won't do this very well unless you also have a supportive *peer* relationship with someone else. If you get interested in Co-Counseling and want to learn to do it, you can pick up any of the magazines here. (There's lots more that I didn't mention—there's *Heritage* for Native Co-Counselors, there's *Colleague* for university and college faculty Co-Counselors, there's *Classroom* for teachers in the primary and secondary schools, and there's a lot of others.) But you won't become a Co-Counselor out of a magazine alone. What you read is interesting, but you need to set up a natural relationship with someone else on a peer basis. Do it with another worker in your field. Do it with a neighbor. Just agree to take turns listening. You'll do it sloppily to begin with—everybody else did that, and I don't know why you should be an exception—but it will get better, and something that you've needed all through your life will begin to become a reality.

I do not say to you that it's "easy." I do say that it's simple, but the simplicity continually gets obscured by the distress itself and by the restimulation which ordinary living piles on us all the time and the lonely little oppressions and the discouragements. It *is simple,* however, and, persisted with, it makes a huge difference in a person's life.

WORTH DOING

Co-Counseling has been outside of Seattle for only eleven years, and it's been a very hectic eleven years. I've worn myself frazzly trying to travel all over and do workshops and lectures and get Co-Counseling Communities started; but it has been very satisfying. In the last few weeks I made a long trip to the East Coast. In two of the workshops I did—one was for Jewish leaders and one was for women leaders—I noticed a phenomenon. A lot of the people at each of those workshops were "old-timers." They were competing a little bit as to seniority. "I've been Co-Counseling nine years," and "I've been in ten"—like that. These people had changed profoundly. This was so plain. These people were in charge of their lives, had complete confidence in their associates, knew what they were about, and were ready to tackle some problems that most of the population is simply too numb with terror to think about, such as the fact that we have to eliminate all nuclear weapons or we're all going to be dead in about twelve years. These people were actually able to think about that. They knew how to discharge their fears and were making plans to insure that their grandchildren had a chance to live.

So I would encourage you to explore Co-Counseling if you can. Explore it through the literature. Do it through participation in the Co-Counseling Community if you can, but if not, use the knowledge that I've reminded you of this morning.

You've always known everything that I've told you this morning, but it's been obscured. Hang onto it and put it to use, and organize it to the extent that with at least one other person you make some kind of commitment to take turns listening, and to try to improve your listening.

It won't work like a magic wand. Just when you start to feel very much better because of your initial successes, you will decide on some level to bring up a deep distress and see if you can handle that, and for a while you'll feel all frazzled because you've got more in the frying pan than you can fry; but, if you persist, life will get more meaningful. You will regain a much better perspective. You will regain again the picture you had when you were young of the way life should be. You will re-acquire some confidence about making your life that way. You will take full advantage of this wonderful, beautiful life that we have a chance to live. You will not live so much of life absorbed by the distress, or let so many days and hours go by in fogs and funks and discouragements and despairs and confusion and terror. You will take charge. More and more you will take charge of your own lives. Just incidentally, you will be much more effective "mental health" workers.

REALLY LIVE

It's our life. We haven't been told that. We've been told the opposite, but our lives belong to us. I sometimes say to advanced students, "There are no 'shoulds' in the universe." Sometimes they look at me with horror and ask, "If I don't have 'shoulds' to guide me in what I do, how will I know I'm doing the right thing?" But there are no "shoulds" in the universe. Your own intelligence is quite satisfactory for guiding your life. You're not obligated to anyone. I thought for years that I was obligated to my children at least, and I couldn't get past that. Then one day, after some Co-Counseling, it occurred to me that anything that my children needed done for them by me, I would do because I wanted to. I didn't have to be obligated.

There are no "shoulds." It's your life. Take charge of it. Have fun.